Parent Warrior

Also by Karen Scalf Linamen

Pillow Talk: The Intimate Marriage from A to Z
Happily Ever After . . . And 21 Other Myths about Family Life
Working Women, Workable Lives with Linda Holland
Deadly Secrets with Keith Wall

Parent Warrior

Protecting Your Children through Prayer

Karen Scalf Linamen

Fleming H. Revell
A Division of Baker Book House Co
Grand Rapids, Michigan 49516

Published by Fleming H. Revell
a division of Baker Book House Company
P.O. Box 6287, Grand Rapids, MI 49516-6287

First printing, February 1999

Previously published under the title *The Parent Warrior: Doing Spiritual Battle for Your Children* by Victor Books

Printed in the United States of America

Library of Congress Cataloging-in-Publication Data

Linamen, Karen Scalf, 1960–
    Parent warrior : protecting your children through prayer / Karen Scalf Linamen.
       p.   cm.
    Originally published: Wheaton, Ill. : Victor Books, c1993.
    ISBN 0-8007-5698-3
    1. Parents—Religious life. 2. Parenting—Religious aspects—Christianity.
3. Parents—Prayer-books and devotions—English. I. Title.
    [BV4529.L55   1999]
    248.3'2'085—dc21   98-31892

For current information about all releases from Baker Book House, visit our web site: http://www.bakerbooks.com

Dedication

This book is dedicated to my parents,
Gene and Geri Scalf.
with much love, appreciation, and respect.
They are parents—and friends—extraordinaire.

Contents

Acknowledgments

I'd like to thank Linda Holland, whose contribution to this book dates back to its conception four years ago! Her insights, encouragement, patience and, above all, friendship bring me great joy.

Friends Jerry and Cherie Spurlock contributed to this book as well: Cherie shared the kinds of personal stories and battlescars only a praying mother of three could offer. Jerry shared insights and also allowed me access to invaluable research he had compiled on prayer. The results of his meticulous research appear throughout this book, particularly in the workbook.

My sister-in-law and friend, Debbie Linamen, shared thought-provoking insights that refined the direction of this book. Her wisdom in spiritual matters has always been great, and I thank God for her!

My grandparents and parents made this book possible through the rich Christian heritage they've given to me. Because of this, I'd like to acknowledge my parents, Gene and Geri Scalf, grandmother Rose Shakarian, grandmother Minnie Scalf, and grandfathers Demos Shakarian and Ronald Scalf, recently gone to be with the Lord. How proud I am of each of you, and how thankful I am of the impact your lives and your faith have had, and continue to have, in my life.

My husband, Larry, deserves not only my thanks, but a clean house and a home-cooked meal as well. Actually, after living through a half-dozen of my book projects and deadlines by now, he probably deserves something more akin to a gold medal and a billion dollars, if the whole truth were to be known. This is because BDC—Book Deadline Countdown—surpasses almost anything known to man or womankind: even PMS is a far second. Yet Larry's faith never wavered. He believed in this project, and he believes in me.

Kaitlyn, of course, was my inspiration for this book, as she is for much of my life.

Above all, I'd like to thank You, God, for letting this book be the first fruit following a very dark season in my life. You have restored much to me—perhaps, in some ways, even more than that which was destroyed. Help me to yield that which remains. For the privilege of life and love and the remarkable joy of plying of my craft in Your service, I am forever grateful.

A Cry for Help

My two-year-old toddled furiously through the house in the throes of a scream. Fortunately for both of us, underscoring that scream were waves of hysterical giggles.

It was easy to see why. Kaitlyn's towheaded cousin, Aaron, was in close pursuit, emitting an even higher decibel level of raucous. Of course, *his* particular noise consisted of a blend of laughter and rather hearty roaring. At the boisterous age of four, a significant purpose in his life remained to scare the tar out of anyone still smaller than he. Adam, just nine months old, watched his brother and cousin with glazed eyes and the drool-ridden fascination reserved for those of us who are allowed to observe life while gnawing on a teething biscuit.

A car door slammed in my driveway. Then another. The kids remained in high gear as I went to the front door to greet my sister-in-law—the mother of Aaron and Adam—returning from a doctor's appointment with the oldest of her three children. I was laughing as I opened the door. "Welcome to the Linamen Zoo!"

My six-year-old niece, blonde and freckled behind a broad smile, bolted inside and headed straight for the commotion and laughter coming from the den.

"Not much wrong with *that* leg," I nodded, referring to the sporadic shin pains that had prompted Ashley and her mother to spend the June afternoon in a doctor's waiting room.

My sister-in-law walked into the living room without a word. She made a beeline for the couch and sat hunched and silent for several heartbeats before her eyes locked onto mine.

They were filled with tears.

"Ashley has cancer," Debbie said. "They want to start chemo right away. She will lose her hair. She will probably lose her leg. And after all that, there is a 50 percent chance that she will die." And then she began to sob.

🍎 🍎 🍎

Our friends Ron and Lisa were stunned when their teenage daughter told them she was three months pregnant by a boy she barely knew. They wrestled with questions about abortion, adoption, or raising the baby themselves. In the end, they let their daughter decide. She chose an unassuming home for unwed mothers, located several hours from her hometown. She left high school. She left home. She would return two weeks before her sixteenth birthday. She would come home a parent.

🍎 🍎 🍎

When Beverly relocated to Ashland, Oregon, with her husband and four children, she had no idea she would later call the experience "the move into hell—literally." Ashland, she soon discovered, is a hotspot for New Age and occult activity. Before long, her son was coming home from school with New Age-oriented "history lessons" teaching him to love "Mother Earth." Each full moon, witches gathered in a public park near Beverly's home for animal sacrifices—the bodies were discovered throughout the city in the following days. Beverly's greatest fear was for her children who, she knew, entered a spiritual battleground each and every day they left her home.

🍎 🍎 🍎

Russ, a friend from my college days and colleague of my husband's, was matter-of-fact when he shared with us—at a football game no less — that he and his wife had reason to believe their three-year-old had been sexually molested by a baby-sitter. As Russ spoke with relative calm, I glanced several rows down the gymnasium bleachers where his daughter, Tasha, was playing dolls with Kaitlyn, then four. When I looked back at Russ, his face was a stolid mask, and I knew it was only the false bravado that kept him from dissolving into tears before our very eyes.

My daughter, Kaitlyn, turned six last month. She got a bicycle for her birthday, and a puppy three weeks later for Christmas. She's missing four baby teeth, believes in the tooth fairy, but is pretty sure that Santa and the Easter Bunny are "just for fun."

Of course, I'm a little more sophisticated when it comes to separating fact from fiction. I stopped believing in the tooth fairy and Santa Claus, oh . . . at least . . . what? Eight or nine years ago?

I'll tell you another myth I've come to recognize. Chances are, you may have grown beyond this one too. It's the myth that, as a parent, I possess the power to fully protect my children from everything that lurks, dark and dangerous and destructive, just beyond my front door.

Maybe I'm idealistic. Maybe I'm just naive. But I used to think I had some control. I used to think my daughter's world would always brim with good things, just because I desperately wanted it to. Of course, that was before my niece was diagnosed with cancer. Before a cousin died with AIDS. Before I started hearing words like "teen pregnancy," "drugs," "occult," "molestation," and even "homosexuality" from the mouths of other parents I knew well.

Without a doubt, the world has always been a dangerous place for children. Unfortunately, just at a time when my children — and possibly yours as well — are most susceptible, the danger zones seem particularly frightening.

What's a Parent to Do?

When confronted with stories like these, it's easy to slip into denial, hanging onto the bald assumption that somehow, someway, it's not going to touch *your* kids.

13

I know that was the way Victor and Bonnie Moore felt. Vic and Bonnie had a Christian home and were in the process of raising three children—the oldest, Ronnie, was a junior in high school. They lived in a quiet suburban neighborhood and were involved in a local church. They thought their family was safe . . . until the evening the phone rang and an anonymous caller spoke the words that shattered their lives.

"Mr. Moore? There's something I think you should know. Your son, Ronnie, is at a party. This party is . . . well . . . the kids have drugs, Mr. Moore. They're dividing and packaging the drugs so they can sell them. Ronnie's heavily involved. I think you'd better get him out—if you can."

Vic thrust the receiver at his wife with instructions to phone the police. Then he tore out of the house, his fist clenched around a piece of paper on which he'd scrawled an address. On his way through the garage, he grabbed a two-by-four. Come hell or high water, he was getting in that house. He was bringing his boy home.

Fifteen minutes later he stood on a darkened front porch, engaged in a shouting match with a young man who refused to open the door. After threatening his way in, Victor rushed into a smoky living room filled with scattering high schoolers. He was vaguely aware of the sounds of water running and toilets flushing as he searched the back bedrooms for his sixteen-year-old son. Vic was still clutching the two-by-four when he found an open window with the screen pushed out.

Victor dropped to his knees. The wooden beam thumped, forgotten, on the carpet. Vic ground his face into his hands and wept. What had he done?

On the surface, Vic and Bonnie may seem to have little in common with Debbie and her husband, Chris, whose six-year-old daughter Ashley was diagnosed with cancer.

Or with Beverly and Ralph, who feared for their three school-aged children exposed daily to New Age and occult philosophies in their public schools and in their community.

Or with Russ and Linda, whose three-year-old began asking to play "games" in the nude—games she had learned from Melinda, her college-aged sitter.

14

But there is a bond. A common denominator. After all, each of these families discovered the hard way that there are dangers in the world today over which we as parents have too little control.

And each of these families found themselves driven, by circumstances beyond their control, to the only recourse which promised any hope at all.

They began to pray.

As Parents, Our Most Powerful Defensive and Offensive Stance Is on Our Knees.

Prayer is a great concept, isn't it? It's conversing with our Creator. It's soul-cleansing and motivating, and it helps us grow spiritually. Prayer can move the hands of heaven, change lives, intercept danger, and impact eternity. It can save marriages, restore relationships and, in some cases, even postpone death.

If we were reading a page of advertising copy describing the "benefits" of prayer, we would find a collection of rather mind-boggling promises that fall just short of offering us whiter teeth, a sexier figure, and the added perk of becoming irresistibly attractive to members of the opposite sex (for *these* promises, please refer to the latest toothpaste, beer, or auto commercials).

The fact is, prayer is associated with nothing but good things. Even more importantly, through His Holy Word God gives us a command — not a suggestion, mind you, but a command — to incorporate this highly beneficial activity called prayer into our daily lives.

Which leads us to a logical question.

Why aren't we praying more?

In preparing for this project, I interviewed a significant number of parents. *Every one* expressed the desire to more fully incorporate prayer into their lives. More importantly, each expressed a need to become more involved in prayer specifically for their children.

Diane, for example, is the mother of a kindergartner and preschooler. She laments: "It seems so many of the values I was raised with aren't important anymore to people. I pray that my kids will say no to temptation, that we'll be good parents, that they'll grow up with the right values. And I pray for their salva-

15

tion. I know I should pray for them every day, but I don't. I get so busy with the day, it's 'catch one when you can.' "

Roger, a professional ball player and father of two, admits his weakness in this area. "A book on praying for my kids? Sometimes I feel I don't know how to pray for them. I'd like to read about ways to find time to do it, examples from other parents, maybe even ideas on how I can let my kids know I'm praying for them. . . ."

My guess is that if I could interview you, your sentiments might not be dissimilar. Are any of us so different? Have any of us "arrived" at the level of "spiritual soldiering" we would like to attain?

I have a confession to make. I did not begin the process of writing this book because I am a prayer warrior. I began writing this book because I wanted to become one.

As a parent, it has been impossible for me not to experience a growing urgency as I see the values—anti-values, really—presented in the media . . . hear horror stories about occult and New Age teachings in public schools . . . read the latest statistics on AIDS or teen suicide or substance abuse. And I find myself wondering, with increasing frequency, how I can protect and raise my kids in a culture gone wild.

The answer—the only answer that makes sense and offers any hope at all—is prayer.

I am convinced that God is calling parents to take up spiritual arms for their children. Indeed, I believe that today's mothers and fathers *must* become impassioned interceders if we are to have any shot at all of raising children who are spiritually, emotionally, physically, and socially whole.

If you're anything like me or many of the parents I know, you may be feeling the same urge. Perhaps you're starting to get a clearer perspective on the dangers of the world in which we live. Perhaps you're tired of feeling stirrings of fear as you read the morning headlines announcing new gang activity in your city or the latest ACLU attack on school prayer. Maybe you're starting to think about the damaging philosophies your children are absorbing every day from even a casual exposure to the media and entertainment industries.

16

Perhaps you have already been faced with a family crisis similar to the ones described earlier in these pages. Or maybe you've been spared—so far—but you're starting to realize that no family is immune.

Whatever your situation, I invite you to join me on a quest. This book began, after all, with my own desire as a parent to enlarge my sphere of protection over my children. Join me on a journey toward a fresh passion for prayer . . . more effective approaches to prayer . . . new power in prayer.

In the following chapters . . .

&. You'll discover the three reasons why a vibrant prayer life is a critical line of defense that today's parents just can't afford to overlook or postpone.

&. You'll benefit from helpful suggestions on how to choose a prayer partner, how to find more time for prayer, how to pray according to God's will, and how to keep your prayers from being hindered.

&. You'll be inspired by real-life stories from the front lines and trenches of spiritual warfare where concerned parents are doing battle for the hearts and souls and lives of their children.

&. Finally, you'll be encouraged to begin your own adventures in prayer with the *Twenty-one-Day Workbook for Parent Warriors* included at the end of this book. The workbook incorporates Bible studies, daily devotionals, and space for you to begin keeping your own prayer journal.

The Parent Warrior was designed to do much more than talk to parents about the benefits of praying for their kids. It was specifically created to *inform, inspire* and, ultimately, to *involve* moms and dads just like you in the powerful practice of effective prayer for their children.

Parent Warriors are made, not born. You can:

learn to take up spiritual arms for your children.

begin to protect, serve, and guide your family through prayer.

discover how to make a difference on your knees.

May God bless you and yours as you begin today to answer the call to battle on behalf of the very hearts, minds, and souls of your children.

PART ONE:
Why Pray?

The Treacherous Times in Which We Live

G erald Garcia doesn't look like a soldier. Fresh-faced and broad-shouldered, he looks much younger than his thirty years. Yet leaning back in his chair, his scuffed Nikes resting atop the second-hand desk in the garage-turned-office of the Young Life clubhouse where he serves as director, he speaks with the wisdom of a battle-scarred veteran.

Gerald's goal is to reach kids in junior and senior high with the life-changing news of Jesus Christ. As a result, he often spends his lunch hours on the campuses of local schools. There he has a chance to visit with teens he has come to know and to meet their friends. He attends ballgames and competitions, often accompanied by his wife, Donna, who is also active in the ministry. He orchestrates off-campus Bible studies, Christian concerts and skits, as well as rock climbing excursions, basketball tournaments, and scuba diving trips. Together, he and Donna work to build relationships with young people, establishing trust and winning the right to be heard on spiritual issues.

This kind of daily—often intense—interaction with junior high and high school students has given Gerald a perspective on teen-life of which not too many adults can boast. He admits, for example, that the kids who attend his Young Life Club are always trying to figure out how he manages to know the things he does about their lives. He explains: "You do this long enough, you get to know enough kids, and you get a pulse of a campus. You know who's into what. You learn what to look for and what the signals mean."

He talks candidly about two sixteen-year-old drug dealers he has come to befriend . . . a thirteen-year-old girl who is involved in the occult . . . the high school senior who is still recoiling from the abortion she underwent so she would have a shot at being voted "Most Beautiful" by her classmates. He recently discovered two thirteen-year-old students having sex behind a campus hedge. Two other junior high girls are self-proclaimed lesbians.

And he speaks so matter-of-factly that you realize these aren't the unusual cases.

I believe there are three reasons why parents *must* learn to pray—effectively, regularly, and with power—for their children. The first reason is obvious. It lurks just beyond our front doors. It can be seen on our school campuses. It loiters around our neighborhoods. And it shouts at us from the TV screens in our living rooms, the silver screens in our local theaters, and through the headphones clamped to the ears of our teenagers.

The first reason is simply and profoundly this: the world in which we are raising our children is fraught with temptations and treachery.

Our children are in danger.

School Zone or War Zone?

In the 1940s, a poll was taken among high school principals and faculty. The educators were asked to list the seven most prevalent problems they faced as educators. Their list? You'd better sit down for these:

1. Talking in class
2. Chewing gum
3. Making noise
4. Running in halls

5. Cutting in line
6. Dress code violations
7. Littering

When the same poll was administered to educators in the '90s, the results looked like something from a Mafia lord's rap sheet:

1. Drug abuse
2. Alcohol abuse
3. Pregnancy
4. Suicide
5. Rape
6. Robbery
7. Assault

Sensationalism? Hardly. Even Ann Landers didn't mince words in a frank reflection on what she termed "our rotting society." She penned these words in a column in which she looked back on some of our "accomplishments" from the year 1992. Her tragic observations are haunting:

> Racism abounds on many campuses across the country. Prejudice against young minorities is on the increase, and I fear it's going to get worse before it gets better.
>
> The war on drugs has turned out to be a colossal failure. The increase in the number of homicides is staggering, and most of it is drug-related. Guns and knives are standard equipment among teenagers. It is not uncommon for a teenager to get shot or stabbed for his jacket or his shoes. Metal detectors in schools help some, but not enough.
>
> While alcohol is still the most abused drug of all, marijuana and stronger substances like crack cocaine are commonplace in junior and senior high schools.
>
> Suicide is the second most frequent cause of death among teenagers in this country. Every 90 seconds, a teenager in America will kill himself.
>
> More bad news is that venereal disease is epidemic, and now there is AIDS, for which there is no vaccine and no cure (*Chicago Tribune*, December 25, 1992).

Many of the dangers listed may surprise us by virtue of their stronghold on the children of our nation. Still, their existence is hardly new news. After all, the temptations of violence, substance abuse, and abused sexual privilege have provided parents with good lecture material since the dawn of mankind. Parents today may not realize the intensity of the pressure to which our children can be exposed, but we are not unfamiliar with the kinds of temptations that often present themselves during teen years, adolescence, and even earlier.

Unfortunately the lures of drugs, sex, and violence, while ever present and ever expanding, are very possibly in the process of being eclipsed by a new source of danger. In fact, hindsight may well identify the more "traditional" social ills as the far lesser of the dangers to which our children are being exposed.

This new attack is subtle. Insidious. It is, in fact, a betrayal because the source of the attack comes in the guise of good intentions, and it comes from within our own ranks of adults who should know better.

Ambushed!

It used to be that parents tried to warn their children about the negative influence of wayward peers: after all, the temptations in their young lives would most likely stem from contact with people their own ages.

The other *adults* who touched their lives — teachers, principals, legislators, authors of children's books and even those responsible for children's television programming — could be counted on in some fashion to uphold and model the values that we, as a society and nation, had embraced for more than 200 years.

Try to re-create this scenario in the 1990s and you'll have a lawsuit on your hands.

It is a simple and unfortunate fact that many of the adults molding the environments, curriculums, and policies impacting today's kids are in the slow but steady process of undermining all that you and I want our children to learn, believe, and become.

We used to warn our children about their peers.

Now it's the grown-ups in their lives that we need to worry about.

Take, for example, the "sensitivity training" that took place during a six-week session of Cornell University's Summer College for high school students in Ithaca, New York. Typically, during these summer sessions high school juniors and seniors can get a "taste" of university life, living on-campus, attending "exploration seminars" that help them decipher career options, and even taking freshman and sophomore level course work for college credit.

During a session in the summer of 1992, however, high schoolers were subjected to a program that went beyond the boundaries of "career planning." The program was designed to enhance their awareness of the feelings and needs of the homosexual community.

Many of the teens were outraged. Others found the information enlightening.

Lynn Minton, in the February 7, 1993, edition of the Dallas Morning News *Parade,* reported on reactions from some of the teens involved.

George, for example, an eighteen-year-old from Pennsylvania, seemed to appreciate the opportunities. He described a "really good" session with homosexual residence advisers. "Some of our residence advisers are homosexual, and they said, 'We're gay, and if you have some questions, you can ask us.' And it was really interesting. I asked them, 'How did it feel to come out?' And how did they know they were gay, and how do they meet each other?"

Eighteen-year-old Rodrigo from Tuscon, Arizona, however, commented on a backlash to the program: "People started complaining about articles in the dorm newsletter, which was edited by the residence advisers. They thought the advisers were a little too pushy in wanting us to understand gay people."

Shemeka Lawrence, a seventeen-year-old Brooklynite, agreed: "Gay people are just a part of everyday life where I come from. It doesn't bother me at all. And the newsletters stressed the idea of accepting people for who they are. But so many of the articles have pertained to homosexuality that I feel the idea is being pressed on us."

The students were also subjected to messages chalked on the sidewalks near their dorms. The phrases included: "We're queer. Does it scare you? If it does, you're going to have to deal with it," and "Queer love is true love too." One girl, after stepping over the message "Are you homophobic?" quipped: "No, but by the time I leave here I will be."

Then there was the commentary of eighteen-year-old Igor, a New York teen who attended the summer session: "A lot of people were angry because of the dorm meeting where we had to pretend. I had to say, 'My name is Igor. I am gay.' And the leader asked questions, for example: 'When was the first time that you became gay?' And people did not want to answer that, because they *weren't* gay, and this made them very uncomfortable."

One of the high school girls went on to observe: "From what I've heard, in the guys' dorm there were a lot of gay men, and I think that bothered [the high school boys] at first . . . before they got to talk to them."

Another student added, "Then some of them [the boys] changed, and some of them remained true to their original feelings."

I am quite certain that when the parents of these teens shelled out $4,100 for their sons and daughters to attend Cornell's Summer College, this wasn't the type of education they had in mind.

An isolated incidence? A freak occurrence? I wish.

Unfortunately, this kind of values assault is more commonplace than we as parents would like to admit—and incidences like this and others are happening even in the most unexpected places.

It's 10 A.M.:
Do You Know What Your Kids Are Learning?

The newest buzzword in educational circles is "affective education," a teaching style that emphasizes the sharing of feelings and emotions in a therapy-like style.

On the surface, affective education programs seem to espouse worthy goals. The programs—in widespread use throughout the nation from kindergarten through senior high—claim to focus on self-esteem, self-awareness, getting in touch with your feelings, decision-making, and dealing with stress. The problem is that the curriculums are based more on psychology than academics.

At a time when illiteracy is rampant and national test scores have never been lower, affective education turns valuable classroom time away from academics and into group counseling sessions. Faculty are being instructed not to teach, but to act as facilitators and therapists, letting the students direct themselves in the expression of their fears, opinions, concerns, and values.

The result is that children are being taught that there are no absolutes. They are encouraged to develop values that work for them, and to rely on their own decision-making skills. In essence, they are instilled with humanistic philosophies via psychological techniques.

Howard Kirschenbaum—who helped create *Quest,* one of the first and most widely distributed effective education programs—based his work on the early experiments of Carl Rogers and Abraham Maslow. Yet W.R. Coulson, who worked closely with Rogers and Maslow as they developed many of these techniques, is one of the most outspoken opponents of the use of psychological techniques in the classroom.

Skills for Adolescence, for example, is marketed as a drug prevention program. Yet Dr. Coulson reports: "When I visted the Skills for Adolescence classroom in San Diego, there was lots of talk of 'I feel' statements. There is no way to explain but to say that students were practicing turning morality into reports of feelings. There was no talk of drugs in the session I observed, and I was told that, by design, there would be none till the last three weeks of the course. Even then the focus would be on subjectivity and decision-making."

Coulson adds, "What happens [with affective education] is that the student's identity is recast. He becomes the subjective center of his own decision making world, no longer an obedient subject of his family's."

Indeed, parents and parental values are cast in a harsh light by many of the programs. In Skills for Adolescence, for example, parents are depicted as bossy, pushy, and nagging; a boy talks back to his parents and isn't disciplined; other stories communicate the concept that teenagers can't talk to their parents.

Coulson admits that Maslow, in fact, came to the conclusion

that "humanistic education preempts parents or silences them. Either way, it leaves children less protected, an easier mark for exploitation."

Indeed, studies have proven that children who go through non-directive, affective education programs are *more likely to begin using drugs* than their nonprogram counterparts. As Coulson explained, "Youthful experimentation with sex, alcohol, marijuana and a variety of other drugs—whatever's popular at the time—has been shown to follow affective education quite predictably; we now know that after these classes, students become more prone to give in to temptation than if they'd never been enrolled."

And yet seemingly educated advocates like Kirschenbaum and others are continuing to foist these philosophies on our public schools. Makers of Skills for Adolescence, one of many such programs, boast of the program's use in more than 8,000 communities and schools throughout the world. Skills for Living, designed for high schoolers, is proported to have reached 600,000 students in more than 2,000 school systems in forty-seven states and seven countries.

Other affective education programs, like Pumsy the Dragon and Duso the Dolphin, attempt to help children relax, deal with stress, think better, and develop better self-esteem through New Age and occult techniques of meditation and guided imagery.

Pumsy the Dragon, for example, is introduced to children between the ages of six and ten. As part of the curriculum, children are led into painting "mind pictures" and chanting.

Duso the Dolpin is the central character in another program, which teaches children relaxation and breathing techniques similar to that used in hypotherapy. The children are then sent on guided fantasies to an imaginary land, accompanied by New Age music. Older children are required to participate in yoga exercises.

All of these are well-founded New Age and occult techniques for getting in touch with "spirit guides," credited with imparting knowledge, inner peace, and enlightenment. Public school educator Dr. Beverly Galyean, in fact, is active in training teachers to help children use these techniques to meet these spirits. "Of course," she remarked at a conference, "we don't call them that in the public schools. We call them imaginary guides."

Thomas Sowell, an economist and senior fellow at Stanford University summed it up well when he said, "There is a whole spectrum of courses and programs designed to brainwash children into rejecting the values, beliefs, and ways of life taught to them by their parents—and to accept the latest fad thinking on subjects ranging from death to sex to social philosophies in general."

More "Stupid Grown-up Tricks"

These acts and others, performed by adults who should know better, deserve to be noted in our nation's Annals of Infamy. But when it comes to—in the revised words of David Letterman—"Stupid Grown-up Tricks," I have my own list of personal favorites.

At the top of my list is the recent decision of officials in Baltimore, Maryland. Recently, the city became the first in the nation to provide Norplant to high school girls at clinics located on the campuses of city schools. Norplant is a controversial, new contraceptive that is surgically implanted beneath the skin on the inside of the upper arm. Once implanted, it diminishes the risk of pregnancy by releasing hormones into the body for five years.

Betsy Hart, former press secretary to the House Republican Policy Committe, believes the American public has every reason to be appalled at the recent decision. "[Imagine] a school administrator allowing a minor to surgically implant hormones in her body without her parents' permission."

Hart adds that the parental consent issue is just the tip of the iceberg. She says that Norplant "woos young women into believing they may recklessly have sex without consequence. While Norplant may prevent unwanted pregnancies, it is no defense against AIDS or other venereal diseases. There also the possibility that Norplant might actually increase sexual activity among teens. Is that what we want?"

In addition, this year alone, the federal government will allocate less than $8 million to programs that encourage our children to abstain from premarital sexual activity—and then turn around and bury those efforts with a whopping *$450 million of our tax dollars* going to promote contraception and "safe sex."

And We Thought Our Biggest Problem Was Helping Our Kids Fend Off a Little Pressure from Their Peers!

There are a lot of powerful books out there outlining today's new danger zones for our kids. It's a topic being discussed on television and radio, in magazines and newspapers, among our friends and in our homes.

It's easy to feel fearful, overwhelmed, and defeated—especially when you exacerbate the current environment with the election of our current President and the immediate fulfillment of some of his promises in support of abortion and the homosexual community. For many traditionalists, the landscape for family values in the '90s—and for the moral and spiritual safety of our children—is a bleak one indeed.

Karen Treeby is a homemaker and mother of two. Like many Christian parents, Karen had a sheltered concept of the kind of world in which she was attempting to raise her children. She knew there were some troublespots, sure. But overall, she anticipated little danger that she couldn't counter with a little churchgoing and Christian teaching at home.

Then one day she heard a radio program hosted by Marlin Maddox. The guest that morning was Dr. Robert Simons, founder of Citizens for Excellence in Education. Her interest peaked; Karen called the Irvine, California-based organization and learned that they had a chapter near her home in Irving, Texas.

Karen began attending CEE monthly meetings in the home of one of the organization's members. There she was exposed, for the first time, to details about programs like Skills for Living, Project Charlie, Pumsy and Duso—programs that were in the very schools her children were attending.

"After that," Karen recalls, "I got scared. I started talking to my husband about private schools for our two oldest kids, who were in first and sixth grade at the time."

After Karen's husband, Ross, attended a CEE meeting he admitted that the problems were real. But he reminded Karen that private school wasn't the answer. The couple simply didn't have that kind of money.

"At that point," Karen remembers, "I was living in fear. I was terrified for my children. And I felt helpless. I prayed for them, sure, but most of my energies were focused on my fear—and on trying to figure out how we could get the money to place them in private Christian schools.

"I remember thinking, *There's no hope. We can't fight it. It's too big. There are too many people in the government trying to take every godly thing out of our schools and our lives.* I was in a state of fear. How were we going to protect our children?"

Raising a family in the '90s can be overwhelming. What's our response? What's *your* response? Do you lean toward inaction and denial? Or do you become frantically energized, hoping that in your shotgun-burst of activity some of your efforts actually hit the mark?

Karen Treeby remembers one woman who attended CEE meetings with a religious fervor. Marie never missed a meeting—in fact, she was a member of several chapters. Marie carried a stack of notes with her everywhere she went. What caught Karen's attention, however, was the fear that radiated from this frail, dark-haired woman. "She was so worried. So defeated. There was no joy in her countenance. The weight of the world was on her. I thought right then, *I don't want to be like her. That's not what God has called me to do and to be. That's not going to help my children.*"

That same week, Ross came to Karen and addressed her drive to pursue private schools for their kids. "Look, hon. Enough is enough. We can't afford private schools right now. You're scared, I understand. But all this is eating you up inside. You've got to let go."

Karen remembers the day she finally took her burden to God in prayer. Ross was at work and the children were at school on the morning that Karen sat in her living room and, crying, began to pray:

"Lord, You know better than I do all the dangers my kids face every day. I used to be so uninformed—and that's not helpful. But now that I know more, I'm . . . I'm scared. And *that's* not going to help my children, either. And so, Lord, here I am. Teach me how to make a difference. Teach me how to pray for them . . . powerful prayers, prayers that can make a difference as they leave my home each morning and go where I can't follow.

"Help me find ways to be consistent in my prayer life . . . to have wisdom in knowing what to pray about . . . to learn what things hinder my prayers so I can use the power and authority I've been given by You. Father, I want to take this thing as far as You will take me. I want my prayers to matter.

"Father, please show me how to pray for my children."

CHAPTER

2

Created to Pray

We can be driven to our knees by what we see in the world around us. We can also be driven to our knees by the intricate design of our own souls.

Created in the very image of God, we were created to pray. God, indeed, wove the need for prayer into the very fabric of our beings. Our communion with the elements of the earth—oxygen, nutrients, and water—enable us to survive and thrive physically; our communion with God in prayer enables our spiritual selves to survive and even thrive.

We might even conclude that prayer is to the soul what breathing is to the body. In prayer, we *exhale* the worries, griefs, and cares of our daily lives; we *inhale* the very presence of God and, with His presence, purpose and comfort, wisdom and strength. Out with the toxins; in with the Life. We become Parent Warriors for our children. We become Parent Warriors for ourselves.

Prayer Meets the Needs of Those Who Pray

As Ronnie's disappearance stretched into weeks, Vic and Bonnie began praying each morning at the breakfast table. As they held hands over bagels and coffee, they reminded God of their absent son. They asked for Ronnie's protection as he wandered lost in the underworld of drug abuse and profiteering. They pled for wisdom. The couple repeated their audience with God each night before they went to bed.

This kind of attention to prayer was new for the Moores. Until Ronnie's disappearance Vic, a salesman, had spent thirty minutes each morning reading Bible passages and self-help/motivational literature. But, by his own admission, his prayer life was pretty "shallow."

When Ronnie disappeared, however, desperation kicked in. Vic and Bonnie realized prayer was the only way they could have any impact at all on the life of their missing teenager. They didn't know where Ronnie was—but God did. And so they met together: Victor, Bonnie, and their Lord, twice a day. It was a pattern that would remain virtually unbroken for months as the couple prayed to see their son restored to health, to his family, and to his faith.

Victor could only trust blindly that his prayers were having an impact on Ronnie. Yet as Victor continued to pray, a strange thing began to happen: his prayers began to have an impact closer to home, in his own heart and soul.

Like a water-starved plant caught in a sudden rainstorm, Vic's withered spirit began to revive. Regardless of what his prayers were doing for Ronnie, his prayers were doing something for Victor!

One Saturday afternoon, Victor sat reading the paper in the den. His youngest son, Mark, sprawled near him on the floor, fiddling with the pieces of a model plane. Suddenly the thirteen-year-old dropped a verbal bomb.

"You know, Dad, you can drink beer and get high, and Ronnie can smoke dope and get high."

Victor stared at his son, feeling a heated response rise in his chest. Sure, Vic had a beer now and then, but he certainly hadn't raised his kids to judge him. Mark knew better than to make a stupid comment like that. Vic opened his mouth, ready to blast Mark, when he took a deep breath instead. Something was telling him to hear Mark out.

"It's not the same, Mark," he said tentatively.

"Sure," Mark said, still fiddling with part of an airplane wing. "People get high, whether you're into beer or marijuana. It's the high people are after."

Vic fell silent. In the long pause, Mark looked up at his dad, startled by the strange response.

Then Vic nodded. "Mark, I believe you're right. And as long as you're in this house, I'll never touch another drop of alcohol."

The battle to quit was a lot harder than Victor had imagined—he hadn't realized how much he depended on alcohol to help him relax. Victor began to wonder what other habits or addictions he had allowed to creep, unnoticed, into his life.

One morning, in prayer, Victor asked the Holy Spirit to reveal any sins he had committed and never confessed. He read 1 John 1:9—"If we confess our sins, He is faithful and just and will forgive us our sins and purify us from all unrighteousness." He opened his heart and mind to the searchlight of the Holy Spirit. He began to recall his harsh words and rebellious deeds that had been buried with time. He remembered the evening, several months before Ronnie's disappearance, when Victor had hit his son. It had only happened once. But once was too often. Other painful memories surfaced as well. Victor began to weep. For three weeks, God refreshed Victor's memory and brought his sins to mind. At the end of three weeks, Victor reread 1 John 1:9 and accepted God's forgiveness for the many things that had been standing between him and his Creator.

As the weeks progressed, there remained no news of Ronnie. But Victor began thirsting for God in a way he had not experienced since he first accepted Jesus Christ in the early '60s. He began to actually enjoy going to church on Sundays. Before long, he added Wednesday evening Bible study to his schedule.

Victor's inner man was thirsty for God—and that thirst had been awakened by prayer.

When Victor first began immersing himself in prayer, he was motivated out of fear for his son. But as his relationship grew with the Lord, he found himself praying for new reasons: Victor needed to pray as much as Ronnie needed his prayers. Suddenly praying for Ronnie was easier. It was enriched. It felt more effective. And it was certainly more intimate.

As the mother of a cancer patient, Debbie too knows what it's like to pray motivated by crisis. She also knows what it's like to pray motivated by a heart that has been awakened to its destiny in prayer.

Debbie remembers: "When I began praying for Ashley, my biggest motivation was seeking healing for my child. But when you spend time with God, you become transformed in the process. Suddenly it's not just for your child. Suddenly I found that this walk with the Lord—this intimacy with the Lord—transcended the fear and pain and agony. In my quiet times—in listening to music, in praise and worship—a double-sided thing took place. Yeah, I was a parent warrior. But I was transformed personally too. There was this thing I was doing as a parent . . . but there was also this thing that was happening just between me and God. In the end, *that's* what kept me praying."

We Were Created to Pray

The Bible is filled with statements, commands, exhortations, and examples that point to our destiny as prayerful beings.

After all, we know that *praying is God's will for us:* "Be joyful always; pray continually; give thanks in all circumstances, for this is God's will for you in Christ Jesus" (1 Thes. 5:16-18).

The Prophet Samuel reminds us that *it is a sin not to pray.* "As for me, far be it from me that I should sin against the Lord by failing to pray for you" (1 Sam. 12:23).

Daniel chose prayer over life: he preferred separation of life from limb in the den of lions rather than separation of his heart and soul from prayerful communion with his Creator (Dan. 6:10-13).

Paul not only prayed, *he recognized his need to be prayed for by others* (Heb. 13:18).

We also know that *Jesus placed a priority on praying.* He prayed for Himself (Luke 6:12-13), He prayed for His disciples (John 17:9), He taught His disciples to pray (Luke 11:1-4), and He corrected His disciples when they tried to hinder His prayers for a cluster of little children (Matt. 19:14).

We pray because our children are in danger; we also pray because we were created to pray. To deny our need for prayer leads to stifled growth, pain, suffering, and even spiritual death.

Studies have shown that newborn children will die if they are deprived of loving communication with a nurturing caretaker. In fact, even the best possible nutrition and the most sterile environment will not save them if warm words and touch are missing from their lives. The need to love and be loved is intrinsic and undeniable. Some psychologists describe this ingrained need for love as a "love tank" placed within each one of us. Children—and even adults—who are denied the kind of communication that would fill their tanks will feel the loss their entire lives.

Prayer meets our need for loving communication with the Caretaker of our souls. Our potential to live prayerful lives is ingrained. If we do not seek to grow into that potential, we will always and forever be vaguely aware of an empty place deep within. We will be haunted by a throbbing void created for a single purpose gone unfulfilled: to contain vibrant and loving communication with our Creator.

CHAPTER

3

Prayer Works

We pray because our children are in danger.

We pray because we were created to pray.

The third dynamic that can send us to our knees is perhaps the most pragmatic of all.

We pray because prayer works. Despite our many doubts and failings, God hears. God answers. God changes circumstances, He changes our children, sometimes He even changes us. Prayer makes a difference. It is worth the time and the effort because prayer accomplishes things that would be "unaccomplishable" through any other means.

Where would we be if we didn't have prayer?

The weeks following Ashley's diagnosis of cancer were filled with a blur of activity despite the fact that the only thing Debbie *felt* like doing was locking the doors, curling up on the couch with her children and pretending her little family wasn't enveloped in crisis. Instead, Debbie and Chris met countless times with doctors . . . Ashley underwent further, often painful, testing . . . Debbie made child-care arrangements for the boys . . . and mother and daughter began the daily, two-hour commute to the Cedar Sinai

Cancer Center in Los Angeles, California.

Several weeks later, exhausted, heartbroken, and humbled by emotional pain, Debbie spent the morning on her knees in her bedroom, pouring out her grief before God. It was hardly the first time she'd spent the morning in prayer. She often met with God in the quiet of the morning after Ashley was in school, Aaron in preschool, and Adam napping soundly down the hall.

But this particular morning, in the wake of a life-threatening prognosis, Debbie's prayers were intense as she cried out for wisdom, strength, and help. The prognosis was too tragic: Debbie feared that, without the intervention of prayer, Ashley would lose her leg and possibly her life. In addition, the emotional pain was too great: without the intervention of prayer, Debbie knew that she couldn't face the ordeal of battling for her daughter's life.

I imagine that in a situation such as this, prayer, even as a placebo, would have some benefit. It could shed some small comfort as it gave the illusion that Someone, somewhere, cared about the suffering of a single family battling cancer in Chino Hills, California.

But prayer is not a placebo. God is not an illusion. And Debbie received more than small comfort. God answered her prayer: He gave her a battle plan.

As Debbie continued to pray, she began to get an idea. Actually, the idea came in the form of images. Images of circles. Protective circles of prayer. Concentric circles of prayer with Ashley safely in the center.

Debbie grabbed a pencil and notebook. Talking through her thoughts aloud with God, she drew a picture of three circles—representing three layers of prayer protection—and began to jot down some of the ideas that were developing in her spirit and mind.

As she pondered her drawing, she thought about the prayers of family and relatives and how these prayers would provide the most intimate circle of protection for Ashley.

As for the middle circle, she thought about the many prayers that would be offered up by close friends and members of the family's home church as they heard the bitter news of Ashley's cancer.

Finally, Debbie was convinced she needed to amass the prayers of a third group: a network of believers who knew of her daughter's need, though they might not know her personally. These prayer warriors would come from friends and acquaintances of those who knew Ashley well. The prayers of this third, more distant group would form a final layer of protection for Ashley and her family as they sought Ashley's healing through spiritual and medical warfare.

Debbie also knew how she would alert everyone. She and Ashley would make prayer-reminder cards. To each card they would tape a picture of Ashley. Each card would also bear the words, written in the wobbly penmanship of the six-year-old: *Please pray for me.*

When Debbie had hit her knees in behalf of her cancer-ridden little girl, she suspected she was in the midst of a spiritual battle for the life of her daughter.

By the time she stood to her feet, she knew she had been handed the battle plans.

What Happens When Parents Pray?

Debbie's prayers made a difference. They enabled her to exhale her fears and inhale comfort, peace, and even a plan of action.

Prayers always make a difference. Sometimes they accomplish the very thing for which we hoped. Sometimes they accomplish a purpose altogether different than the one we held most dear.

When we pray for our children, a frequent prayer is that God would either change a child, or change a set of circumstances surrounding a child. Victor's prayer was that God would change his son Ronnie. Debbie's prayer was that God would change the circumstances of Ashley's disease. These were the obvious benefits that committed, praying parents hoped to bring to fruition through their prayers.

I believe, however, that our prayers can harvest a diverse array of benefits. Prayer can, in fact, create *layers* of benefits in our lives. Some are obvious; others are subtle. But prayer works because, regardless of the specific nature of the changes it brings, it always renders our lives enriched in some way.

How does prayer work? Sometimes by surprise. Sometimes it works because it brings about a benefit or a change that is utterly unexpected.

What can happen when you begin to pray fervently for your children? Your prayers can change your child, of course. But here are some of the other benefits you may begin to experience:

Your prayers can change you.

We've already seen how Victor's prayers for Ronnie began to bear fruit in Victor's life. Regardless of how God would deal with Ronnie, Victor's spirit was revived, renewed, and refreshed as he picked up spiritual arms as a parent warrior for his son.

Bill is another parent whose prayers brought an unexpected change in his own life.

When Bill's son, Alan, began to "hang" with some tough crowds in their downtown neighborhood, Bill hit his knees in prayer. For weeks he asked God to protect Alan, then fourteen. Bill knew that the long-hours of his job, and the fact that his wife worked full time too, left Alan unsupervised five afternoons a week and some evenings as well.

Bill brought his concerns regularly to God in prayer, looking for a change in Alan, perhaps even a change in Alan's choice of friends. What he didn't expect was that God would begin to change Bill. The more Bill prayed, the more he felt God calling him to reprioritize his life. He shared his feelings with his wife, and their prayers together began to confirm the feeling. Bill asked his company for a transfer, and the family put their home on the market.

Within six months they had relocated to the Midwest. Housing was less expensive and Bill's wife decided to work part time, arriving home just before Alan came home from school. Bill began to spend evenings and weekends with his children as they explored the fishing holes near their new home. The neighborhood was quieter too. Oh, sure, there's drugs and trouble in any neighborhood—but this time, Bill was going to be around to help guide Alan away from the danger zones.

If you are not willing to experience God's breath of change in your own heart and soul, don't bother praying for your children.

Prayer works—and the first place it works is in the life of the man or woman who cares enough to pray.

Your prayers can change circumstances.

Buzz Moody was hardly a prayer warrior. As a relatively new believer, she knew how to pray for her meals and how to ask God for things and that was about it. She had never prayed aloud in a group. Prayer, in fact, seemed a rather intimidating concept.

Buzz heard about Moms in Touch just about the time her daughter, Lindsey, was beginning high school. Moms in Touch, founded by Fern Nichols in 1984, began as a grassroots network of praying mothers. Nearly ten years later, Moms in Touch has inspired dads, grandparents, and even college students to answer the call to prayer. There are approximately 22,000 Moms in Touch groups throughout the world, with contacts in forty-one countries. Each group consists of two or more mothers with children attending the same school. Members meet for an hour each week—usually in someone's home—to pray for their children, their children's peers, and teachers and administrators of the school the children attend.

With Lindsey facing adolescent challenges in a public high school, it seemed like the right time for Buzz to take another look at the benefits and power of prayer. She began attending the Moms in Touch chapter near her home.

Buzz admits that, like Vic and Bill, her new prayer life changed *her* before it wrought major changes in Lindsey's life. She explains, "My relationship with God was the first thing to change. I came to know Him much better—I even began to trust Him with things I used to try to take care of myself. My faith grew too—first as I saw God answering the prayers of the other mothers in my group, and then as I saw Him answering my own prayers."

For two years, Buzz prayed that Lindsey would find and spend time with Christian peers: people who didn't drink or do drugs. When Lindsey made the cheerleading squad, Buzz began to pray for the other girls on the squad. Later, she and the other mothers in her chapter began to pray for the student body officers.

By the time Lindsey began her senior year, all the girls on the cheerleading team, save one, were believers. And every student body officer—from the president down—were Christians too . . . and at a public high school, no less!

Prayer had altered circumstances that directly impacted the quality of Lindsey's life. During Lindsey's junior and senior years, Buzz found her prayers changing. By now, Lindsey knew how to pick Christian friends, and Buzz began to pray, instead, for godly characteristics that she wanted to see developed in Lindsey.

Buzz knew that prayer had changed her own heart and her own relationship with God. Her prayers had also impacted an entire school. Now she wanted her prayers to change her daughter.

Your prayers can change your child.
Renee Sims attended Moms in Touch with Buzz. She frequently encouraged Buzz in her prayers for godly traits in Lindsey. After all, Renee knew, firsthand, how prayers could change a child.

When Renee's son Buddy began his freshman year, he was shy and withdrawn. Renee—and the other mothers in the group—began to ask God to develop—of all things—boldness in the quiet boy. When Buddy found out about the women's prayers, he objected. "Mom, tell your friends to stop praying like that! It's not going to help!"

Yet over the course of his high school career, Buddy began to grow in the very manner for which his mother and her friends had so long prayed! He began to talk with his friends about God. He shared Christ with several teachers. As a senior, he even talked a teacher into letting him do a report on the authenticity of the Bible. The controversial report generated even more opportunity to talk about God with his peers.

Never underestimate the power of prayer. God orders the hearts of even pagan kings and rulers—He can make a difference in the heart of your child.

Finally, your prayers can teach your children how to pray.
Mark and Nancy Bellinger are praying parents. Sometimes they pray together. Frequently they pray at separate moments during

their busy days. Sometimes they pray as a family. Often they pray alone.

But kids are sharp. They watch. And they learn.

One Saturday Nancy got a call from a woman in her church whose sister, Margaret, was suffering from a skin disorder that left her hands and arms covered with severe sores and blemishes. That evening, Nancy, accompanied by her five-year-old daughter Cherie, went with her friend to pray for Margaret at her home. Margaret, thirtysomething and frail, smiled appreciatively as her sister and Nancy stood behind her in the kitchen, tenderly grasped her bandaged hands, and began to pray to God on her behalf.

The next night Margaret agreed to attend Sunday evening service with her sister. After the service, the sanctuary was filled with informal activity as friends visited, kids roamed the aisles, and families began to make their way to the parking lot. Margaret stood chatting with Nancy when suddenly a small figure darted close and tugged on the older woman's skirt.

Margaret looked down into the face of five-year-old Cherie, who had brought with her two other children. "Well hello, sweetie," Margaret crooned.

"Hi. I brought two of my friends," Cherie annouced, still grasping Margaret's skirt. "We want to pray for you."

Nancy watched, her heart brimming with awe and joy, as Margaret extended her hands and Cherie led her two friends in gently grasping the bandages. Then the five-year-old prayed aloud, her tender voice clear as a tiny bell, reaching the very gates of heaven with its heartfelt chime.

As he wrote to the Philippians, Paul pointed to himself as a model and an example for his spiritual children, encouraging them with the words: "Whatever you have learned or received or heard from me, or seen in me—put it into practice. And the God of peace will be with you" (Phil. 4:9).

As parents, perhaps we need to keep this verse in mind, as much for our own sakes as our children's! Our children *will* follow our examples, whether we want them to or not!

I remember one of my many power struggles with Kaitlyn. She was four at the time, and I have no idea now what the struggle was over—I only know that we were enmeshed in a disciplinary war. I spanked her, then asked if she were willing to cooperate. She said no. I spanked again, asked again. She stomped and shook her head! I sat her on my lap, tried to reason with her, asked for her cooperation again, and she yelled NO! I spanked again, she cried, I asked again for her cooperation, and she defied me yet again.

This had gone on nearly half an hour when, her face streaked with tears and a defiant glare in her eyes, my four-year-old shook her finger at me and raged, "I've just about had it with you!"

I managed to keep a straight face—barely. But later, after our conflict had resolved in a hug, I remembered her words. They were uncomfortably familiar. They were, in fact, the very words—finger-wagging and all—that I frequently used on her!

Wow! Is that how she perceived me? Stubborn, rageful even, pointing my finger and spouting threats? I felt convicted as I heard my tone and my words—"I've just about had it with you!"—mirrored back to me by my child.

Remember the poignant commercial, aired back in the days when we were growing up, in which a small son mirrored all the actions of the father he obviously worshiped? Their day was filled with Norman Rockwell scenes of fishing, kicking a can along a dusty road—and regardless of the activity, a bright-eyed little boy watched and copied meticulously. Right about then, of course, the father lit up a cigarette. The little boy knew better than to follow suit—then. But he watched, nevertheless. And he learned.

Our children learn by our examples. My dad used to joke with my sisters and me, saying, "Do as I say, not as I do." It was a joke because he knew as well as anyone that we would do precisely as he did, regardless of his words to us. Our actions speak louder than our words.

Do you want your children to experience a vibrant, empowered communication with their Creator?

Then show them what it's like.

PART TWO:
How to Put More Prayer into Your Parenting

CHAPTER 4

Making Time to Pray

For parents like Karen Treeby, Chris and Debbie, and even Vic and Bonnie, becoming stirred to prayer leads inevitably to questions about the most effective way to go about actually doing it.

After being called to spiritual arms by the unique circumstances facing each of their families, these parents found ways to weave prayer into the very fabric of their daily lives.

Yet notice the diversity!

ᐧᐧ After spending hours in solitary prayer, Debbie felt the Holy Spirit directing her to amass prayer support on behalf of Ashley. Mother and daughter spent an afternoon making 250 prayer reminder cards, which Debbie then began distributing to friends and family.

ᐧᐧ Vic and Bonnie continued praying together, as a couple, each morning and evening.

ᐧᐧ Karen Treeby and Buzz Moody were looking for more structured support. They each joined Moms in Touch chapters near their homes.

There are myriad ways to personalize your prayer life to meet the demands of your schedule and the needs of your family.

But every custom plan begins at the same place, with the same intitial investment.

Every plan requires a commitment of *time*.

So Many Good Intentions . . . So Little Time
When it comes to prayer, good intentions seem aplenty. But finding the time to accommodate these intentions is another story.

If finding time for prayer in your life sounds like a good plot for a "Mission: Impossible" espisode, consider these statistics:

❧ The average adult, in a lifetime, will have wasted an accumulated total of three years doing nothing but watching television commercials!

❧ That same adult, in his or her lifetime, will have spent more than *2,000 hours* waiting for meals in restaurants and fast-food establishments.

❧ *Forty-three work weeks* will be spent reading junk mail delivered by the post office! That means by my retirement, junk mail will have consumed nearly one year of my life, assuming that I read from 8 to 5 every workday, breaking an hour a day to eat, rest my eyes, and wash the newsprint from my hands!

We find time for so many trivial pursuits in our lives!

Yet each and every one of us, at some point in our lives, has fallen into the trap of using "lack of time" as our justification for a less-than-prolific prayer life.

Numbers like these drive home the fact that, as a society, we are fairly capable of finding time for the activities we *really want* to include in our lives.

And so we take a deep breath and ask ourselves the inevitable and the uncomfortable: Do we really want to pray? "Want to" with our very hearts and souls? Because if we do—if we *really* want to, finding time to pray will not be a stumbling block. It will merely be a matter of logistics.

Is Your Problem Lack of Time . . . or Lack of Priority?
There is a difference between wanting something with your *heart* and with your *head*. We all know people, for example, who want a

good relationship with their spouses. Yet if career constantly tops the priority chart in their lives, we can safely assume that the value they place on their marriage comes from their intellect, not their heart.

And of course, we all know (perhaps far too well!) people who say they want to start exercising and get in shape! And yet when months and years roll by and the only thing changing shape is the easy chair by the TV, we begin to suspect that the source of the good intention is, once again, the head and not the heart.

I know people who want to pray for their kids. They want to have an eternal impact in the lives of their children. Yet moving from a "head want" to a "heart want"—making prayer a heartfelt priority—isn't always a natural process.

In a previous chapter we examined some of the external dangers that can motivate us to pray. Yet being motived from the *outside in* is not nearly as effective as becoming motivated from the *inside out*.

Which leads us to a natural question. What *is* going on in our hearts? How do we make praying for our children a priority in our lives? What is motivating us internally? What *should* be motivating us internally?

I believe there are four primary ways that we can develop an inner motivation that will enable us to place prayer at the top of our priority list:

Growing into discipline.

There are a lot of disciplines—prayer, of course, is a discipline—that we neglect when we are immature and grow to appreciate as we mature. Healthful eating might be one example. Exercise or good sleeping patterns might be others.

If you have been fortunate, solid Bible teaching, good childhood training, and wise role models may have helped you mature into a man or woman for whom prayer is a natural priority. It happened without strain or stress. There was no epiphany of revelation or flash of insight. Good prayer habits simply grew on you as you grew into maturity.

If this is your situation, you have been blessed with a wonderful heritage. Ingrained habit is an effective internal motivator.

Graduating from the school of 911.
There are, however, many of us who were not fortunate enough
to grow naturally into prayer warriorship. For those of us who are
not so blessed, an emergency can function as the catalyst that
propels us into heartfelt spiritual warfare. It's the threat that drives
us; the scare that brings us to a place of action.

Two weeks ago on a Sunday afternoon I experienced a strange
sensation in my left arm: it suddenly went numb from shoulder to
fingertips. I mentioned the oddity to Larry and then went back to
whatever I was doing at the time. Half an hour later, the numb-
ness had yet to recede. I called a weekend-care clinic, spoke with a
nurse . . . and was instructed to get to a hospital emergency ward
as soon as possible. She mentioned the words "unstable angina"
and asked if there was someone who could drive me.

Three hours, one EKG and 200 dollars later, I was released.
The doctor suspected a pinched nerve. I was relieved, but still
shaken by my close call. It seems melodramatic in hindsight, but I
can't forget the fear that had me crying in the lobby, waiting for
an admitting nurse and wondering if I'd get to stick around long
enough to finish raising my child.

And guess what I did this week? Bought a new headset for my
Walkman and finally began that exercise program I've been prom-
ising myself for the past half-dozen years. My "heart attack"
turned out to be a false alarm. But it was real enough to motivate
me to action.

Emergency, fear, and crisis. Vic and Bonnie know what it's like
to have a tragic turn of events change the way you think about
prayer. It's not the gentlest transition into spiritual warfare, but it
works in a pinch.

Making an investment of your time.
It's a circular equation: If you care deeply enough about something, you will find the time to make it happen. And in reverse
logic, if you invest enough time and energy into something, you
will find yourself learning to care.

The Bible says it succinctly in Matthew 6:21: "Where your
treasure is, there your heart will be also." And what, after all, is

more treasured in the fast-paced '90s than time? Where you invest your time, your heart will be also.

You can see this principle illustrated every day, in your own life, in the lives of people around you, even in the media. After all, how many movies have been created around themes like these?

A man and woman—who share a mutual disgust for each other—are thrown together via an adventure, crisis, or quest. At the end of the movie, they've invested enough time and energy in each other that they've managed to fall passionately in love.

A cynical adult gets talked into linking up with a rebellious, unlovable kid. After months of struggles, hostile verbal exchanges, disappointments, and hopeful moments, a friendship is forged that leaves the audience reaching for their Kleenex.

Like me, you may have seen the movie *Sister Act* in which Whoopi Goldberg plays a woman forced to live in a convent to escape detection—and termination—by the former boyfriend who also happens to be an underworld kingpin. A former nightclub singer, when she enters the convent she is testy, bored, and sarcastic. But by the end of the movie her investment of time with the nuns—even though it was against her will—has changed her heart. After identifying her Mafia-connected boyfriend for the police, the character cries at the prospect of leaving her friends in the black and white habits. This particular plot hit the big screen in 1992, but the theme is as old as the hills.

Where your investment is, your heart will follow.

Begin to make time for prayer—regardless of how you feel or how busy or distracted your life may be—and before long your heart will catch up.

Letting love drive your prayers.

Maybe you were raised to appreciate the value of prayer. Perhaps a crisis has spurred you to your knees. Or there's a chance that you have simply willed yourself to invest the time in prayer.

Of course, these motivations are not mutually exclusive—you might find yourself driven by one, a pair, or all three. But I believe that—to give parent warriorship the kind of priority that it deserves in your life—any combination of motivations *must* include love.

There's no doubt. We are complex creatures and can be internally driven by many emotions. We can be motived by guilt, greed, anger, compassion, duty, patriotism, self-interest, self-preservation.

But, love. Wow. Now *there's* a motivator.

Remember back to your courting days? If you were like me, nothing beat the power of a relationship when it came to motivating you to lose weight, work out, earn money for weekend dates, or take a crash course in some special interest or hobby of your beloved.

In high school I fell madly in love with a kid named David Thornton. We were sixteen and he was quarterback of his high school football team. Football? Having no brothers, I was only vaguely familiar with the sport. But suddenly my interest piqued. I bought a book on football and studied it like my life depended on it. Our relationship was the catalyst for my discovery that an end run wasn't caused by a snag in the toe of my nylons and that tight ends weren't just something found on the beach or at the gym.

Love is urgent. Demanding. Consuming. It takes priority—and creates priority—like little else in our lives can manage to do. And when it's all said and done, I believe that nothing can beat love when it comes to getting us—and keeping us—on our knees for our children.

After all, doing spiritual battle for our children isn't just about logistics—it goes far beyond matters of when, where, why, and how to pray. It's about love. It's about our relationship with God and our relationship with our children and standing at the intersection of the two. There is enormous power in the crosscurrents of the love we share with our Creator and the love we share with those we create, and it is this energy, this synergy of love that can, indeed, drive parent warriorship to the top of our list of priorities.

If you've made prayer a priority in your heart, finding time to pray may still take work, but it will happen! When our heart's desire is to pray—and pray for our children—our busy schedules will be challenges, but they will no longer have the power to keep us from impacting our children, their worlds, and their eternity through our intercession.

Finding Time to Pray

Several months into Ashley's chemotherapy, Debbie was exhausted. Without any notice, Ashley's treatment had had the effect of adding a forty-hour workweek to Debbie's already busy shedule. After spending eight to twelve hours a day, three to six days a week, negotiating the logistics of treatment, Debbie still needed to find time to meet the needs of the other members of her family. She needed time to recoup from the emotional drain caused by the life-threatening diagnosis. And she needed time to pray.

Debbie knew that the difficulty she faced in finding time to pray for Ashley—much less for her sons Aaron and Adam—was not an excuse for misplaced priorities. She had examined and reorganized her heart. More than ever before, she knew that parent warriorship was truly a priority in her life.

Now all she needed to do was find a way to conquer the clock.

Making time to pray—and making a habit of it—isn't easy, especially in these fast-paced days of phones, FAX, and Federal Express. Distractions abound! Yet with some planning and forethought, we can begin to set aside the time we need to make a difference with our prayers.

Real People . . . Real Solutions

If you think that your personal pattern of prayer needs to correspond with that of your best friend, your pastor, your parents, or even your spouse, think again. Of course, there are benefits to praying in sync with a partner, which we will examine later. But we do ourselves a great disservice when we compare ourselves to others and try to live their lives.

The important thing is that you incorporate time in your life to pray. The following examples are taken from the lives of real people who tackled the very real problem of finding time for prayer . . . and, as you will note, no two came up with the same solution!

ᴥ Mark and Nancy Bellinger, for example, are the proud parents of a son and daughter: Craig, twenty-four, Kristen, twenty-two, and Cherie, now seven. For these Southern California parents, finding time to pray is a very individualized process.

Mark takes time each morning after breakfast to kneel beside the living room couch and pray for his family. Nancy, on the other hand, doesn't have a set time for prayer. She instead manages to work it in quite thoroughly throughout the day.

"I still take time to pray," she explained during a phone conversation, "but just not all in one lump. I believe you can pray while you're working, driving, cooking . . . you can be cleaning a room and praying. It's not like a chore. God gives you a joy when you pray."

To help Nancy maintain an attitude of prayer during her busy daily schedule, she listens to praise and worship music at home and in her car. "It helps focus me and keeps my mind open to prayer," she says. "I feel like a lot of my life is devoted to prayer."

≈ Carol Bartosh, mother of four, combines two disciplines in one. Every morning by 9, she puts on sweatpants and Reeboks and steps out her front door. Carol lives across the street from me, and in the nine months my husband and I have lived in Duncanville, Texas, I've seen her pumping past my house innumerable times, walking at a clip I'd be hard pressed to maintain at a jog! She wears a blue headband. She works up a sweat. And she's out there rain or shine.

I used to admire her for her commitment to fitness. I admire her even more having recently discovered that her commitment is coupled with a devotion to prayer. Carol uses this hour each morning to walk for fitness, and also to walk with God. These are her moments when she talks to Him about her family, bringing the needs of each child — and her husband, Tom — before the Creator of the universe.

≈ Hillary, on the other hand, is a single mother raising two elementary-school-aged boys. When going through a bitter divorce and custody battle, she developed the habit of fasting and praying one day a week for her sons. Three years later, the pattern continues.

≈ Finally, Ron and Christine have recently entered the fraternity of parenthood with the birth of their daughter. Sarah is three months old, but their joint prayers for her date back to her very conception.

"Throughout Christine's pregnancy," Ron says, "we prayed every night together. Sometimes I put my hand on her stomach as we prayed. Christine is diabetic, so it was a high-risk pregnancy, and our prayers began as we petitioned God for Chris' health and the health of our baby. As the months progressed, our prayers did too. We prayed that our baby would grow up to know and love God as much as we did."

He adds: "Praying every evening—together—has become a habit we look forward to. It draws us closer . . . it keeps us accountable . . . and I know we'll both be better parents because of our commitment to this time we've set aside to spend with each other and with God."

Targeting a Time That Works for You

When it comes to identifying and protecting a prayer time that is appropriate for your lifestyle and schedule, there are enough "strikes" against you already—so it's important that you don't sabotage your own efforts by trying to maintain a prayer time that is incompatible with your personal body clock!

My husband is the Dean of the College of Business at Dallas Baptist University. As an educator, he frequently teaches students about principles of personal efficiency. One of the concepts that he advocates is for men and women to "tune in" to their personal body clocks.

People are "wound" to very individualized schedules. Some people, for example, like to greet their day with brainwork. Their minds are fresh and rested and they feel energized to tackle quiet activities that require concentration. Other people prefer mindless busywork in the morning until they've had a chance to wake up mentally, usually somewhere around lunch.

In corporate settings, people are learning to work with—not against—their natural "bent." Researchers and scientists are telling us that, on a very individualized basis, we simply do better at some tasks at certain hours. Why not take this into consideration when planning our quiet times with God?

I, for example, struggled for a long time with the misconception that I am somehow, spiritually, a second-class citizen if I do not engage in quiet time that takes place somewhere in the chronological vicinity of dawn. Unfortunately, I am not a morning person. Once I had to get up at 5 in the morning to take someone to the airport, and I considered borrowing an alarm clock for the task. Of course, I *have* an alarm clock, but mine has never been exposed to single-digit A.M. numbers and I see no reason to break a very agreeable tradition.

I don't even write well in the morning. Several years ago I was cowriting a book while working full time as an editor with Focus on the Family. In order to meet our deadline, I started dragging myself into my office at 6:30 in the morning so I could write for a good hour before my colleagues came in and it was time to shift to my Focus projects. Unfortunately, more often than not I ended up asleep, face down, on my computer keyboard. As 8 o'clock approached and I heard the first voices in the reception area, I would jolt awake and, blinking, try my best to look awake and productive.

Months after the book was done, I admitted this embarrassing pattern to friend and coworker Scotty Sawyer. I assumed I had pulled off my charade and that my colleagues never knew I'd been sleeping at my desk before work hours. That's when Scotty told me they *all* knew.

My mouth hung open. "But how? . . ."

Scotty shrugged good-naturedly. "When you'd been asleep, you'd have a keyboard imprint on your cheek."

Luckily, I have come to terms with my own body clock. And while I've always admired morning prayer warriors, I no longer aspire to join their ranks. After all, I soon discovered that by trying to establish an early morning time for prayer, I am unwittingly setting myself up for failure. For me, it is far better to find other—later—times when my closed eyelids have a shot at representing something other than the fact that I am in deep slumber.

Put Your Time Where Your Mouth Is

What is your body clock telling you? When are you most prepared to spend quiet—and alert—moments with God on behalf of your family? If you aren't sure, take a moment to take stock several times throughout the day. Ask yourself how you are feeling and what kinds of tasks you feel you might successfully accomplish at that time. Are you alert? Distracted? Sleepy? Energized? Do you feel like interacting with people? Tackling paperwork? Could you read something thought-provoking, like devotional literature? Could you concentrate on prayer?

Once you are better aware of your personal patterns of energy and concentration, take a mental walk though a typical day and note some of the slower periods in your schedule that might accommodate some time spent with God.

When you are done, look for opportunities in your schedule

Having examined my personal "body clock time," I am typically at my best in the ☐ early mornings / ☐ mornings / ☐ afternoons / ☐ evenings / ☐ late night (you may need to check more than one box).

Considering my current daily schedule, I am more likely to find some flexible, discretionary time in the ☐ early mornings / ☐ mornings / ☐ afternoons / ☐ evenings / ☐ late night.

Taking both of the above factors into consideration, a good time for me to meet with God—a time when I can be alert and relaxed—is the following:

Time: _____

Place: _____

I will be using this time for the purpose of praying for my child(ren) (include name or names here):

_____

_____

_____

---

that are compatible with body-clock times conducive to concentration and communication with God. For example, evenings after the kids are in bed might provide an opportunity for quiet time, but you may be too exhausted to couple that quiet time with the emotional energy for effective prayer. Perhaps afternoons or mornings are a better match.

Select a time when you can faithfully come before God on behalf of your children daily or even five days a week. Later, as you begin the workbook section of this book, you will be asked to make a formal commitment to this time. Right now it is enough to identify a time that will work for you.

Remember, by matching moments when you have the time with moments when you have the desire, you will have created the best possible environment for the development of effective — and maintainable — patterns of prayer!

Finding a Prayer Partner

When I was growing up, my favorite time to pray was late at night, when my sisters were asleep and my parents had either gone to bed, or perhaps were on the final dregs of a late-night movie or news show before turning in for the evening.

Sometimes I would lay in bed and pray. Often I would kneel by the side of my bed. Many times I laid face down on the carpet and poured out my heart before the Lord. There's a sweetness in our intimate moments with God alone. To be sure, a vibrant prayer life is built on exchanges such as these.

And yet there is no denying that God wants us to bring other people into our prayer life, whether we are praying for ourselves, friends, spouses, our country, or our children. Jesus Christ makes this clear in Matthew 18:19-20 when He instructs that "if two of you on earth agree about anything you ask for, it will be done for you by My Father in heaven. For where two or three come together in My name, there am I with them."

I know that each of us has participated in corporate prayer in church services, before meals, in school chapels. In fact, I recently had a chance to take part in a moment of corporate prayer at the opening of—of all things—a rodeo I attended with my family here in Texas.

But take another look at Matthew 18:19. Note the implied intimacy. The verse specifies numbers. And those numbers are small. Real small.

In a group of two or three, there's no hiding among the crowd. You can't fade into the woodwork. And, in a small group, it's a lot harder to let your mind roam to planning dinner, rebuilding the car engine, or redecorating your living room. Of course, because groups of two and three are so intimate, they can be threatening too.

And yet, when we pray in small groups—baring our souls and our secrets, our fears and our joys—we are enriched in ways that we cannot experience when we pray alone, and certainly are not likely to attain through the brief and formalized prayers of large masses.

Benefits of Praying Together
To begin with, praying regularly with another person or a small group can keep you praying.
It's called accountability.

I like the frank comment of my friend Cherie Spurlock. The mother of two boys and a girl—a teen, adolescent, and kindergartner—Cherie meets weekly with a friend from church for the express purpose of praying for their children. Sheri also doesn't mince words: "Face it! We're lazy and we just don't do it," she told me rather matter-of-factly one day over the phone. "On our own, we get distracted by the jillion and one things going on in our lives. At least for me, knowing that a friend is coming over today at 1, for example, helps me to budget my time and *really* spend that time praying specifically for the kids."

Praying regularly with another person or a small group also develops intimacy.
In our fast-paced lives, there's so little opportunity for intimacy, isn't there? So few chances for intimate connection with another

human being. Instead, we make time for projects and activities and all the things on our "to do" lists. We make time for work and for laundry and for television and for cooking and even for church. But even church—where everyone is dressed in their Sunday best, sitting among a crowd, listening to a sermon pumped through a loudspeaker—is not intimate.

And yet, intimacy is so important. After all, as Charles Swindoll observed during one of his radio broadcasts, we impress people at a distance . . . but we impact them one on one.

We crave that kind of impact, don't we? In our marriages, with our friends, with our children, in our churches, with God, we are hungry for intimacy. And yet we continue to pack our schedules with the kinds of circumstances that sabotage closeness. We rush around, we worship in large packs, and we work hard to keep our conversations on a superficial level that masks our truest feelings and deepest pain.

Several months ago, I agreed to teach a new evening Bible study at our church. In the beginning, I admit that I was a little disappointed by the size of the group—each week, between five and eight women meet in the fellowship hall for a two-hour session that includes prayer, reviewing our answers to a home Bible study lesson, and a brief lecture which I give.

Now I look back on my initial disappointment, and I shake my head.

In a larger group, it would have been unwieldy to go for coffee and pie after the Bible study, or to meet before work in the morning for breakfast. In a larger group, it would have been so much easier to maintain sterling images and hands-off facades. And in a larger group, we probably wouldn't have begun sharing the kinds of intimate prayer requests that allowed acquaintance to develop into friendship.

Now, when I think about the members of our small group, I am familiar with at least one personal struggle, temptation, or disappointment that each woman has shared—and they know some of mine, as well. We encourage each other and pray for one another—real prayers about real needs. And it simply couldn't have happened in a larger group.

Third, praying regularly with another person or a small group enables us to express to each other the power of God's unconditional love and acceptance.

When a friend shared with me that she struggled with a cigarette addiction left over from her pre-Christian days, she did so with tears in her eyes. "I'm such a bad person," she told me. "I can hardly bear to go to church—I'm so afraid that someone will find out that I smoke and realize how horrible I am. I don't belong there—I don't know how God puts up with me."

Another woman, whom I'll call Gail, was slow to tell people about a traumatic family crisis. Gail's son, Scott, had been active in church and youth groups since he was small. He'd attended a Christian college, sung in the church choir, and dated a Christian girl. There had been no clues whatsoever to prepare his parents for the afternoon he stood in the kitchen and announced that he was gay, that he had AIDS, and that he was dying. Gail admits that in the beginning, she was afraid to tell other believers what her family was facing. She was afraid of judgment and rejection.

When we share intimately in prayer, there is, unfortunately, always the possibility that someone will recoil, appalled: "Your son has *what?*" Or even to condemn: "Did you say *cigarettes?*" And yet there is no better opportunity for each of us to practice being like Christ, mirroring His unconditional love for those who hurt or struggle.

There is healing when we share our deepest secret with a prayer partner, and that partner still loves us. When that happens, it's a littler easier to believe that God, who we can't see, can love us that way too.

Finally, praying regularly with another person or a small group can give us the opportunity to experience God's love in a physical, tangible manner.

I know what it's like, when praying by myself, to almost feel the arms of God giving me a hug at a moment when I need it most. But sometimes that's not enough, is it?

Last week I picked my daughter up a few minutes late from school. After claiming Kaitlyn and her friend from the "pick-up" point for tardy mothers and car-pool drivers, I popped my head into the kindergarten classroom to wave a greeting to Debbie Sims, Kaitlyn's teacher.

Debbie looked up and smiled. It was a feeble smile.

"You OK?" I queried. "You look tired or something."

"Oh, just one of those days," she admitted. Then she sighed. "You might pray for me, if you think about it. In a few minutes I'm having a meeting with a parent . . . and it's going to be a tough one."

I nodded, then turned to go. My hand was on the classroom doorknob when I turned and retraced my steps. Quickly, I wrapped my arms around Debbie's shoulders and prayed aloud for God to give her wisdom and strength and sense of renewal in her spirit. Then I gave her a big hug and started to leave again.

"Thank you," she said softly. "I really needed that," she said. There were tears in her eyes. But then, there were tears in mine too.

I imagine that Mary, Jesus's mother, knew what it was like to get a hug from God. In the early years, it might well have been a hug from a God with small grubby hands and a dead frog in the front pocket of his tunic—ah, but what a hug. There were others, like Mary, during the life of Christ who knew what it was like to get a touch—a real touch—from God Himself.

Perhaps, with a little help from our friends, we can know what it feels like too.

Characteristics of a Good Prayer Partner

The person you choose as a prayer partner can enrich or detract from your time together in prayer, so it is important to put some thought into your selection. This is particularly true if you will be praying about highly personal or confidential issues! Not every believer is mature enough to handle the sensitive issues in your life and in the lives of your children in a godly manner.

When I am considering a prayer partner, I keep the following guidelines in mind. Remember, these are guidelines, not laws. How cautious you are in selecting a partner depends on the nature of the matters you'll be sharing in prayer. Selecting someone with whom to pray regarding your son's grade point average, for example, will require much less caution than the selection of someone with whom to pray regarding your daughter's addiction or your son's homosexual lifestyle.

With this in mind, consider teaming up with someone who demonstrates the following traits.

Vulnerability and transparency.

One day I received a phone call from a close friend I'll call Laura. She was crying. "I need to ask your forgiveness," she blurted through her tears. "I've done something really awful."

She went on to tell me about a conversation she'd had that morning with another woman from her church. Laura, struggling with an attraction to a married man, had decided to approach a godly woman and friend and ask if they could pray together about her struggle. She'd spent the morning at the home of this friend, where she had tentatively broached the subject.

"I didn't know how to bring up the matter," Laura confessed to me over the phone. "Then I remembered that you had written an article on this subject, and that you once had a similar experience. So I mentioned this to my friend as a way of explaining what I was feeling, and. . . ."

Laura's sobs broke anew. "I'm really sorry. I never should have mentioned your article or your experience. I didn't even mention your name, but this other woman got really angry anyway. She said I shouldn't have mentioned anyone else. She said I was gossiping. She said I needed to ask your forgiveness. She said she couldn't believe I'd talk about someone else like that. I felt so humiliated and embarrassed. I left as soon as I could, but driving home, I began to think she was right. I had to call you right away. I'm so sorry . . . can you ever forgive me?"

"Laura, did she ever say anything about your struggle? You told her you were struggling. Did she ever talk about that?"

Laura was still tearful. "N . . . no. All she talked about was how horrible I was for gossiping."

Laura's friend had created an effective smokescreen — at Laura's expense! Unable to cope with Laura's pain and transparency, this friend had diverted the encounter onto "safer" ground, judging and convicting Laura for "gossiping" rather than dealing with the greater issue. "How" Laura had shared her story, rather than "what" Laura was sharing, had become the focus. The deeper — and more important issue — had been sidestepped neatly.

When looking for someone with whom to share the more vulnerable aspects of our lives, it's important to select someone who knows what it's like to feel vulnerable! Someone who understood how scary it is to bare a soul would never have reacted in that manner to Laura.

Later Laura acknowledged that, in all their relationship, this friend had never shared anything vulnerable or intimate from her own life. This could have been Laura's first clue that this woman might panic when faced with Laura's vulnerability and transparency.

The cross sharing of vulnerability is crucial in the development of intimacy — and praying with someone about your heartfelt needs, concerns, and fears is, if anything, intimate!

Psychotherapist Novlyn Hinson has shared that, even in therapy, the exchange of transparency can build trust and intimacy. She explains: "Sometimes, if I am faced with a client who is struggling to open up and talk about his issues, I'll drop my guard a little. I'll share something from my own life. As I become transparent, I've entrusted him with something intimate from my own life. He may feel, in turn, that I can be trusted with his transparency, as well."

I do this in my friendships at times. If I sense that a friend is burdened about something — that she isn't sure that she can talk to me about it — I'll look for an opportunity to share something personal of my own. It sounds manipulative — and it could be, if the message I am sending by my transparency were a lie. But it's not. By my transparency, I am saying — and with all sincerity — "Our friendship is a safe place in which to share burdens. I can trust you with this personal part of my life . . . and you can trust me too."

Confidentiality.
Colleen is a good friend who brims with entertaining tales from the lives of other people, some of whom I know, most of whom I

have never met. There is nothing malicious in her stories — she just can't keep a secret.

One night Larry and I were driving home from an evening with Colleen and her husband when Larry spoke the words that were on my mind as well: "Gee, I wonder if she talks about us behind *our* backs?"

I have shared personal issues with Colleen, and we've prayed together about struggles in her life and in mine. But in choosing what personal issues to share with Colleen, I keep in mind the fact that while Colleen has many wonderful traits, confidentiality might not be one of them!

Don't set yourself up for disillusionment, embarrassment, and even bitterness by sharing highly sensitive prayer concerns with friends who may not be discreet with your problems. Look for discretion in the prayer partner with whom you choose to share your more intimate concerns. By the same token, when someone shares something sensitive with you, remember the need for discretion. Private matters shared before God in prayer are not for the public ear!

Solid theological footing.

When selecting a prayer partner, look for someone with a solid, working knowledge of the Bible. Someone with obvious theological misperceptions may be prone to cause more confusion than good!

One of my friends, for example, believes that nothing in the Old Testament applies to Christians today; another has bought into the "name it, claim it" philosophy that wealth and riches are due every believer just for the asking. When my mother-in-law was stricken with cancer, someone told her that she must have some unconfessed sin in her life. Still another friend has swung to the other extreme, believing that miracles and healings are no longer among God's options for Christians today.

When we pray, our prayers are most effective when they are in sync with God's Word and His will — choose a prayer partner whose prayers can reflect the character and nature of the God we serve.

Repentant spirit and desire to live pure before God.

We each have sinned . . . and we continue to struggle with the temptation to sin. Yet sin that remains unconfessed and unforgiven in our lives will hinder our prayers. When selecting a prayer partner, be aware of areas of unconfessed sin in her life. One woman I know is living with her boyfriend—we pray together, but our prayers are usually centered around issues in her life. I suspect that the rebellion in her life renders her less than effective when it comes to interceding. In the future, as this friend deals with her heart and regains a right relationship with God, she may well become a powerful prayer warrior. The conquest of our darkest sides and deepest struggles, after all, is the fodder which God uses to nurture great spiritual growth and insights. But today, at this juncture in her life, this friend is someone I can pray with and for. I might also choose other prayer partners who can help me intercede for my family.

Working knowledge of prayer.

If possible, choose someone who prays and who is familiar with the power of prayer. Another option is to select, as a prayer partner, someone who has not, in the past, spent a lot of time in prayer, but who has a desire to incorporate more prayer into his or her life. In this respect, you and your partner can keep each other accountable in your shared goal to spend more time in prayer.

Choosing a Prayer Partner

Where can you find someone with whom you can share your prayer life? The possibilities are endless, and they begin right in your own home.

Praying with a spouse.

In their book, *If Two Shall Agree* (Grand Rapids: Baker/Revell, 1992), Carey Moore and Pam Rosewell Moore talk about the adventure they embarked on when they began, in the days of their courtship and through the early years of their marriage, to pray together every day.

The Moores give numerous reasons why a husband and wife who are believers might want to incorporate joint prayer into their busy lives. One reason is simply that it makes for a better marriage.

As one woman, quoted in their book, observed: "We have never seen a couple we knew, one who prayed together regularly, encounter serious marital difficulties. It's that simple . . . and yet that profound."

Pam writes:

> We do not make it a daily prayer that God will protect our marriage from prevailing danger, but we do make it a frequent one. We bring our vows to mind in a number of ways. Sometimes we repeat our formal marriage commitment to each other to remind us of our binding promise. At other times I look at Carey's wedding ring and rehearse privately the promise I made when I placed it on his finger.
>
> We two disciples remember another disciple who failed the Lord when he was sure he would not. "I'll never deny You, Lord!" Peter promised. But Peter broke his promise, and we remind ourselves of the warning Jesus gave him, "Watch and pray, so that you will not enter into temptation."

Carey writes about a woman who prays with her husband twice a day—after breakfast and before bed—as a way of making Christ the center of their home. He then adds:

> To place Christ at the center of our homes means, of course, to tell Him, "You are our God," not just at prayer time but all day long. I cannot be careless or insensitive in what I say to Pam and then pray with her. Nor can either of us treat anyone else rudely or engage in gossip and criticism, or allow conceit and pride to rule our relations with others, and expect God to hear our prayers at the end of the day.

What a wonderful thought it is that, in addition to all the other benefits of praying with someone, we might strengthen our marriages as well! And especially for parents who want to impact their children's lives through prayer, it is wise to remember that a strong marriage is one of the best possible gifts we can give our children.

After all, our marriages help shape the emotional and psychological development of our children.

Our marriages also provide the blueprints for what our children will look for and expect from their own marriages.

Finally, our marriages set the tone in our homes, creating the environment in which our children will either be drawn to spiritual things by our examples, or driven away from God.

Praying with a small group.

Buzz Moody's daughter Lindsey recently graduated from high school. Buzz remains in association with Moms in Touch—this time as the leader of a MIT chapter at the elementary school where her youngest daughter—and my daughter, Kaitlyn—attend. Moms in Touch is one of the options for parents in search of a small group environment. (For information about MIT, or to join or start a chapter near your home, write Moms in Touch, P.O. Box 1120, Poway, CA 92074 or call 1-800-949-MOMS.)

Friends, Dan and Kathy Hamer, whose son suffers with a condition doctors are still trying to diagnose, found small group support when they began to attend a prayer group for parents of chronically ill children.

Small group prayer can be organized around any common ground. You can probably name a dozen parents with whom you have something in common—perhaps you all have preschoolers, or are raising your children as single parents, or are battling substance abuse in the life of one of your children. Some of these parents might grasp at the idea of joining you, in your home or theirs, for prayer on behalf of your and their children.

Praying with a friend.

Before she began praying with friend Cindy Beaton, Cherie Spurlock had heard about Moms in Touch and considered joining. Instead, she and Cindy decided to tailor a weekly prayer time that was better suited to their schedules and their particular needs. Their friendship had served as the foundation for their time together in prayer—and yet before long, their time together in prayer became the foundation for an even deeper friendship.

According to Cherie, one of the many benefits of this kind of arrangement has been the insights shared between mothers in prayer.

"It really helps to have someone else's input," she admits. "Because Cindy's kids are older than mine, she's been through a lot of what I'm going through and what I'm praying about. It's been a big help. And even though I've never been exactly where she is in terms of raising her family, I somehow am able to contribute as well. There are times, for example, when you are praying that the Lord simply drops an idea or insight in your mind. Cindy has said to me, following some of our prayers, 'In all my years of praying for Lori and Lance, I've never thought to pray about it the way you did.' Sometimes she calls me on the phone during the week and says, 'You'd never believe what happened . . .' and shares a development that has come out of the new perspectives we gained in prayer."

Another woman that I interviewed—I'll call her Rebecca—talked about the prayer partnership that she has been privileged to share with a close friend. These friends don't have an established time at which they meet to pray. In fact, their busy schedules mean that months may go by without a good heart-to-heart talk, much less a chance to pray together. And yet these friends have managed to stay close and stay abreast of the transitions, crises, challenges, and dramas in each of their lives, and to uplift each other in prayer through thick and thin.

"It might be months between conversations," Rebecca explains, "and yet this friend always cuts through the superficial and gets right to the heart of things—'How are you *really* doing?' she'll ask, and I'll know she wants the truth. She knows me—the good, the bad, and the ugly—almost better than anyone because we've been honest with each other and we've really prayed for each other.

"And what means a lot to me is that it isn't a one-sided relationship. A long time ago I went through a hard time and Pamela helped pray me through the experience. Then, several years later, Pamela had an experience similar to mine. We prayed together over that too. It's give and take, give and take. During one crisis she's strong for me, and hopefully I can be strong for her during the next one."

Turning Good Intentions into Action

Who might join you in prayer? Who, in your life, shares the common grounds of a belief in God, a desire to pray, and a burden for the children of this generation? Who might accompany you as you journey together into effectiveness as a true parent warrior?

At the end of chapter 4 you identified a workable time and place for you to conduct your personal prayer life. It might be feasible for a prayer partner to join you at this time and place. For example, if you meet daily with God at 6:30 A.M., it might be possible for a spouse or friend to join you once a week at that time. It is more likely, however, that you will find yourself and your partner selecting a new time—one that works best for both schedules. My suggestion is that—however you manage the logistics—you attempt to keep a daily personal appointment with God, while finding a partner with whom to pray at least once a week.

Take a moment and provide the answers to the following questions and statements:

How often would I be interested in praying with a partner?
_____

Three people with whom I would feel comfortable praying are:
1. _____
2. _____
3. _____

Their phone numbers are:
1. _____
2. _____
3. _____

Call this person—now, if possible. Arrange a time—at your home, at a park, over lunch, during a break at work—to spend a few moments sharing concerns and then taking these concerns, together, to the Lord.

I have spoken with _____,
who has agreed to join me in prayer as parent warriors. Our first appointment with God in prayer is scheduled for:

Date: _____
Time: _____
Place: _____

In world where dangers and temptations abound . . . in a time when Christian-bashing is the politically correct thing to do . . . in a society where facades and schedules inhibit intimacy—it is our Father's desire that we come together in fellowship and prayer. And it's easy to see why. The risks of intimacy are always intimidating . . . but the rewards are great. Whether we pray with spouses or relatives or friends, in intimate clusters at church, on lunch breaks, over the phone or in each others' homes, we really do need each other.

CHAPTER
6

Praying According to the Will of God

I was driving Kaitlyn to school one morning when I had the idea to pray with my kindergartner about a problem that was looming on the horizon for our little family. It was a problem that she had been very disturbed about, and I thought getting her to pray about it might bring her—and me—some comfort.

We were being asked to move from a home we had been renting for six months. This was to be our third move in less than a year: we were ready for something permanent! Before moving to Texas, we had owned our own place in California. We wanted to live in our own home again—and we had exactly one month to find our dream home and close escrow.

We had been living in Texas for nine months, and our experiences renting homes had been dubious, at best. The first home we had rented was supposed to be long-term—we signed a year's lease, paid our rent promptly, and had been there three months when we got a notice from an out-of-state bank: it seems our landlord had been pocketing our rent without paying the mortgage. He had, in fact, skipped town—the house was being repossessed, and we had thirty days to get out.

We rented another house, month to month, from the father of a friend, with the agreement that we would be moving as soon as we found a home to buy. We found one six months later—a rustic three-story that we dubbed the Treehouse. We began negotiations and, when they looked positive, we gave a tentative two-month notice. Now, just as our bid had fallen through, our landlord had made arrangements with new renters, and we had a month to move—even though we had nowhere to go.

I could see that the constant transition had been taking its toll on Kaitlyn. She often asked where we would go and who we could stay with if we didn't find a house to buy. She worried about her toys—where would they go when we moved?

We were still several miles from her school when I took her hand. "Kaitlyn, I know you've been worried about moving. Let's talk to God about it. I know He'll take care of us and give us someplace good to go. Do you want to pray?"

Her eyes lit up. "Let's ask Him to give us the Treehouse! He could make those people change their minds!"

I chewed my lip. "Well, yes . . . technically. You're right, God could make that happen. He can do anything. But I'm not sure that's what we should pray for."

Her smile dimmed. "But that's what I *want* to pray for."

I read once that we need to pray about our problems, not pray for solutions. Thinking back through the years, I can remember far too many times when my prayers have focused, not on giving my problem to God, but on telling God how I want Him to solve my dilemma. Instead of praying, for example: "Lord, You know I need to find a job—show me the position *You* want me to have," I approach Him with: "God, *this* is the job I want. Please help me get *this* one."

I had worked hard to revise my own prayer life—I wasn't about to let Kaitlyn fall into my old bad habit.

Driving south on Spur 408, I talked to her about man's wisdom versus God's wisdom—in terms I hoped a five-year-old could understand. When we finally prayed, I realized there was nothing wrong with her understanding—she understood, in fact, better than I had for many years of my adult life.

"Dear Jesus," she squeezed her eyes shut as we sped along. "I really hope You give us the Treehouse. But I'm really just supposed to tell You that we need a place to live. Soon. It might be the Treehouse. Or it might be another house. Or it might be an apartment, or maybe even a hotel. I know that wherever You decide to put us, it'll be the right place, and You'll take care of us. Wherever that is. You'll come up with something. I love You. Amen."

That afternoon, when I picked Kaitlyn up from school, we had an errand to run before going home. We were going to see a house. *Another* house. By then we'd seen what seemed like hundreds. They'd all been deadends. All except the Treehouse. It had taken us six months to find that one . . . and now I had a matter of days to find something else. It was tedious. It seemed hopeless. I was surprised my friend and realtor, Bonnie Rea, was even still speaking to me after all I'd put her through.

As soon as we drove up, I knew it was The House. Windchimes danced on a sweeping, southern front porch. I could almost taste the lemonade and hear the creak of rocking chairs. Inside, Kaitlyn picked out her bedroom within the first two minutes. In the next five, she discovered a playhouse in the backyard. When it was time to go, I had to drag her off the property.

Negotiations were over in a week. We moved in four weeks later.

We were sitting on the porch—our porch—when I pulled Kaitlyn onto my lap and gave her a hug. "I want you to remember something," I told her, twirling her ponytail around one finger.

"What."

"It's something I want you to remember always."

"OK."

"Do you remember the first day we saw this house?"

She nodded.

"Do you remember what we did that morning? In the car? When I was driving you to school?"

She pursed her lips, then smiled. "Was that when we prayed?"

"That's when *you* prayed. You told God we needed a place to go, remember? You said He could pick the place—it didn't even need to be the Treehouse. You'd let Him pick. Your job was just to talk to Him about our problem. Remember?"

"I 'member."

"He heard you, Kaitlyn. He heard you, and He brought us to this house that afternoon. *That afternoon!*"

"He really heard me."

"Remember that always."

"OK."

"Always?"

"Always, Mama."

"You Ask and Do Not Receive, because You Ask Amiss"

It would have been so easy, driving in the car, to pray according to *our* will that day. And what would God have done with our prayer then? Given us a house He knew would be second best for our needs? Or given us the place He wanted us to have, leaving a kindergartner to wonder why her prayer for something called a Treehouse didn't get answered?

When it comes to praying for anything—and especially when praying for something as precious and irreplaceable as our own children—our best bet to getting our prayers heard and answered is to *pray in accordance with God's perfect will.*

I believe there are several ways we can make sure that we are praying in accordance with God's will and not our own. The first, of course, is to give God the problem—not *our* solution to the problem. This is important because many times we simply don't know what God's will might be in a particular situation. Sometimes choosing between "neutral" things like homes or even jobs can leave us in a quandary. Which is why we need to present God with our *dilemma*—rather than ask Him to rubber-stamp His approval on our *solution* and to use His divine power to somehow magically bring about the manifestation of *our* wills.

Why is it necessary to base our prayers on God's will rather than our own? It seems redundant, to begin with, to pray for something we know God wants to give us anyway. And it certainly goes against our selfish human nature at times—there are so many things we want God to do *our* way. Why *not* pray according to our wants and our solutions rather than God's?

One reason is that praying for God's will—and having God's will manifested in our lives because of our prayers—is appropriate simply because God is God. Isaiah 55:8 reminds us that: " 'For My thoughts are not your thoughts, neither are your ways My ways,' declares the Lord."

But on a more selfish level, praying for God's will is to our benefit, as well. Romans 8:28 makes that clear enough as Paul writes: "And we know that in all things God works for the good of those who love Him, who have been called according to His purpose."

And what better way to be called according to His purpose than to reflect that great purpose in our prayers.

Praying According to God's Will As It Is Revealed in Scripture

Sometimes, as in the example of the house, we don't know what God's will is for our lives, and in these circumstances we need to practice giving God our problems, not our version of the solution.

There are times, however, when we can know *exactly* what God wants for us. Knowing the desire of God's heart in these matters, we can approach Him boldly in prayer, telling Him not only about our problem, but reminding Him confidently of the solution that we know is well within His perfect will for us.

This is possible, of course, because God's Holy Word gives us an inside look into the heart, mind, and will of God.

When we pray in sync with Scripture, we can be confident that we are praying in sync with God's will for our lives.

If I am faced with a sticky situation at work where standing up for right will cost me politically or even financially, I don't need to wrestle with whether I should act with integrity or whether I should compromise the truth and save my skin. I already know what God's will is for me: Proverbs 4:23-27 instructs me to "above all else, guard your heart, for it is the wellspring of life. Put away perversity from your mouth; keep corrupt talk far from your lips. Let your eyes look straight ahead, fix your gaze directly before you. Make level paths for your feet and take only ways that are firm. Do not swerve to the right or the left; keep your foot from evil."

If I, before marriage or as a divorced and single parent, become romantically involved with a nonbeliever, I don't need to ask God what His will for my heart and for my life is. I already know, because Paul in 2 Corinthians 6:14 has made it clear: "Do not be yoked together with unbelievers. For what do righteousness and wickedness have in common? Or what fellowship can light have with darkness?"

Praying According to Scripture by Praying in Scripture

Just as I can use the Scriptures to know God's will for my life—and to pray accordingly—I can use the Scriptures to know what God's will is in the life of my children.

One of the very best ways I can do this is to incorporate God's Holy Word *verbatim* into my prayers for my children.

Take, for example, Paul's prayer for his spriritual children in Hebrews 13:20-21: "May the God of peace, who through the blood of the eternal covenant brought back from the dead our Lord Jesus, that great Shepherd of the sheep, equip you with everything good for doing His will, and may He work in us what is pleasing to Him, through Jesus Christ, to whom be glory forever and ever. Amen."

What a powerful prayer to adapt—virtually verbatim—for my own children!

Dear Heavenly Father, I know that You are the God of peace who brought up our Lord Jesus Christ from the dead. I ask that You equip Kaitlyn with everything she needs to do Your will. I ask that You would fashion her and work in her so that her life is pleasing to You, and that You would do these things through Jesus Christ, to whom be glory forever and ever. Amen.

I might even add, according to Romans 12:2: *Father, I ask that Kaitlyn would not be conformed to this world, but that she would be transformed by the renewing of her mind, that she might prove what is Your good and acceptable and perfect will in her life.*

And on another day I might choose to pray from 2 Timothy

2:22: Father, please give Kaitlyn the strength to flee youthful lusts. Give her the desire to pursue righteousness, faith, love, and peace with those who call on the Lord out of a pure heart.

What powerful prayers! And I can have every confidence, as I pray, that these requests are reaching the ear of God because they represent the very will of God for my children.

Why Pray Using Scripture?
I think there are at least four benefits of invoking the power of Scripture in our prayers.

As we have already mentioned, praying in God's own words gives us the confidence that we are praying according to the will of God. And when we have this confidence, we can also be sure that He will answer our prayers. First John 5:14-15 makes this very clear. "This is the assurance we have in approaching God: that if we ask anything according to His will, He hears us. And if we know that He hears us—whatever we ask—we know that we have what we asked of Him." What a fantastic promise!

Praying in God's own words can build our faith.
We all know that faith is an important dynamic when it comes to having God hear—and answer—our prayers. And where does faith come from? "Faith comes from hearing the message, and the message is heard through the word of Christ" (Rom. 10:17). The word of Christ! By repeating God's own words back to Him when we pray, we can strengthen our faith even as we speak.

There is power in the written and spoken word of God.
Hebrews 4:12 reminds us that "The Word of God is living and active. Sharper than any double-edged sword, it penetrates even to dividing soul and spirit, joints and marrow; it judges the thoughts and attitudes of the heart." And in Isaiah 55:10-11 God promises that "As the rain and the snow come down from heaven, and do not return to it without watering the earth and making it bud and flourish . . . so is My word that goes out from My mouth: it will not return to Me empty, but will accomplish what I desire and

achieve the purpose for which I sent it."

And for whom did God send His Word? For us. He sent it for you and for me, and for our children and our children's children. It was sent for us, and it was sent to profit us: "All Scripture is God-breathed and is useful for teaching, rebuking, correcting and training in righteousness, so that the man of God [parent of God] may be thoroughly equipped for every good work" (2 Tim. 3:16).

The Word of God is *powerful*. It is alive, it always accomplishes that which God wills for us, and it will prosper and profit those of us who incorporate it into our lives.

Praying in God's own words helps us fulfill God's will for our lives. God desires for His Holy Word to become an intricate part of the fabric of our lives.

In education, there are certain concepts that, if they are considered important enough, are integrated "across the curriculum." A positive example of this can be found in Christian private schools and universities. Before he advanced into more administrative duties at a Christian institution of higher education, my husband taught business classes. It was, of course, expected that faith and prayer and godly character would be discussed in, say, one of the school's many theology courses. But at the schools Larry has associated with—Biola University and now Dallas Baptist University—faith in God is considered important enough that Christian precepts are incorporated into classes spanning the curriculum. That means regardless of the course and the teacher, there is a place to talk about God's Word and how it applies to business, math, communication, literature, nursing, and so on.

When Paul encouraged believers to "Let the Word of Christ dwell in you richly in all wisdom," I don't think he intended that we should limit our integration of the Word into our lives. I believe God's Word is crucial enough to span the curriculum of our busy days. In our parenting, in our workplaces, in our discussions with each other, in our quiet times, and in our prayers—and especially our prayers for our children—we are enriched when we incorporate the power of God's Word.

Incorporating Scripture into Your Prayers

We'll be doing more of this in the following workbook. But let's not wait until then to put this important principle into practice! Take a moment to ponder the following Scriptures. The following verses are taken from prayers that Paul uttered on behalf of his spiritual children—the new believers he had the privilege of leading into a saving knowledge of Jesus Christ. What beautiful templates for us to use as we pray for our own children!

In addition, these verses examine character traits that God desires for every believer to incorporate in his or her life. You can be sure that it is God's will for your child to develop these godly traits as well.

After you review each segment of Scripture, rewrite it in the form of a prayer to God, revising the verses just enough to insert the name of your son or daughter where appropriate. When you are through, take a moment to offer these powerful words to God in prayer.

2 Corinthians 13:7, 9, 11

"Now we pray to God that you will not do anything wrong. Not that people will see that we have stood the test but that you will do what is right even though we may seem to have failed. . . . We are glad whenever we are weak but you are strong; and our prayer is for your perfection. . . . Aim for perfection, listen to my appeal, be of one mind, live in peace. And the God of love and peace will be with you."

Your turn:

Dear Father, I pray to You that my child, _____, do no wrong; not that I, as a parent, might look good, but so that _____ will learn to do what is right, regardless of how I might appear! Father, I also pray that _____ be made perfect in You. That he/she would strive for perfection in You, would be open-minded to receive instruction in spiritual things, and would live in peace. I also pray that You—the God of love and peace—would be with him/her always.

Praying According to the Will of God

ᴥ Ephesians 1:15-19

"I have not stopped giving thanks for you, remembering you in my prayers. I keep asking that the God of our Lord Jesus Christ, the glorious Father, may give you the Spirit of wisdom and revelation, so that you may know Him better. I pray also that the eyes of your heart may be enlightened in order that you may know the hope to which He has called you, the riches of His glorious inheritance in the saints, and His incomparably great power for us who believe."

Your turn:

_____

_____

_____

_____ .

ᴥ Ephesians 3:14-19

"For this reason I kneel before the Father. . . . I pray that out of His glorious riches He may strengthen you with power through His Spirit in your inner being, so that Christ may dwell in your hearts through faith. And I pray that you, being rooted and established in love, may have power, together with all the saints, to grasp how wide and long and high and deep is the love of Christ, and to know this love that surpasses knowledge—that you may be filled to the measure of all the fullness of God."

Your turn:

_____

_____

_____

_____

_____

_____

_____ .

CHAPTER

7

Ways Your Prayers
Can Be Hindered

When I ran into an old college friend at the city post office, I expected an easy exchange of trivia about kids, spouses, and jobs. What I heard instead were the sketchy details of a frightening legal drama in which the stakes appeared to be the physical and emotional well-being of two little boys, ages five and seven.

Tall and lanky, with jet black hair and friendly features, Bill Smith looked drained as he spoke about recent choices made by his wife of nine years. It seemed that Rhonda had suddenly tired of married life and moved in with a fifteen-year-old girl named Cindi, a former prostitute the Smiths had met through a church outreach. Rhonda had taken up drinking and smoking and blue language. She hadn't made any attempt to see her sons in over two months. Currently, she was living with the man who supplied drugs to Cindi and other children like her.

Standing beside a gleaming wall of P.O. boxes, Bill wrestled with possible reasons for the nightmarish transformation in Rhonda's personality and lifestyle. He talked about the fact that for years Rhonda had suffered with a physical disorder which

85

caused occasional seizures and required constant medication. Had her illness "set off" this bizarre relay of choices? Or perhaps there was demonic influence at play. She had seemed a happy person, a committed spouse, and devoted mother for too long to consider it all an act. So what had caused the breakdown? His questions were reasonable. He wanted to know *why*.

Not, of course, that he had much time to ponder. His days and nights were spent working full time, single-parenting his five- and seven-year-old boys, and meeting with lawyers to discuss the custody battle.

He'd just learned that Rhonda wanted the children.

She was suing for custody.

For Bill, the two years following our chance meeting at the post office would be a nightmarish blur of domestic crises, legal battles, and spiritual warfare. At the time we spoke, Bill could only guess at what the future held. But one thing was certain: he was going to do everything in his power to make sure that his sons stayed with him, in a God-fearing home.

An important part of his arsenal was prayer. And an important aspect of prayer was searching his own heart and soul for anything that would stand between his requests and God's answers to those requests.

Bill admitted: "When a marriage falls apart, there's never a totally innocent party. Looking back, I can see where I made some mistakes, and I've confessed these mistakes to God. I'm also trying hard not to let hatred and bitterness take root—although that's easier said than done. The important thing right now is for me to keep my walk with the Lord pure. I don't want my sin standing in the way of my prayers for my boys. The stakes are far too high to allow that to happen."

Preparing for Spiritual Battle

Like an athlete training for a contest or a soldier preparing for a skirmish, when we prepare to do spiritual battle for our families, there are things that we can do that will enhance our chances at success.

Of course, we can't manipulate the final outcome of our prayers.

Regardless of our preparation, there are times that God's answer to our prayers will be much different than we expected as He tells us *no, wait,* or even *I've got something very different in mind for that particular problem.*

I don't ever want to try to second-guess God. But I also want to make sure that I do everything in my power to present my petitions to Him effectively, without allowing anything in my life to thwart my prayers.

The Bible tells us that there are a number of things that can hinder our prayers from even reaching the ears of God. Hindering factors appear to fall into six major categories:

Unforgiveness.
"And when you stand praying, if you hold anything against anyone, forgive him, so that your Father in heaven may forgive you your sins" (Mark 11:25-26).

Sin and disobedience.
"If I had cherished sin in my heart, the Lord would not have listened" (Ps. 66:18).

"If anyone turns a deaf ear to the law, even his prayers are destestable" (Prov. 28:9).

Not obeying God's will for our relationships with our spouses.
"Wives, in the same way be submissive to your husbands so that, if any of them do not believe the Word, they may be won over without talk by the behavior of their wives, when they see the purity and reverence of your lives. . . . Husbands, in the same way be considerate as you live with your wives, and treat them with respect as the weaker partner and as heirs with you of the gracious gift of life, so that nothing will hinder your prayers" (1 Peter 3:1-2, 7).

Selfishness.
"When you ask, you do not receive, because you ask with wrong motives, that you may spend what you get on your pleasures" (James 4:3).

Inhumanity.

"If a man shuts his ears to the cry of the poor, he too will cry out and not be answered" (Prov. 21:13).

Pride.

"The Pharisee stood up and prayed about himself: 'God, I thank You that I am not like all other men — robbers, evildoers, adulterers — or even like this tax collector. I fast twice a week and give a tenth of all I get.'

"But the tax collector stood at a distance. He would not even look up to heaven, but beat his breast and said, 'God, have mercy on me, a sinner.' I tell you that this man, rather than the other, went home justified before God" (Luke 18:11-14).

Checklist for Effective Prayer

There are many promises concerning prayer in the Bible. What too many people conveniently forget, however, is that many of these promises have conditions attached to them! In several passages, God outlines for us certain things which can disqualify our prayers, hinder our requests from reaching the ears of God, or hinder God's response to our prayers.

Jerry Spurlock is an adjunct faculty member at Dallas Baptist University. He is also a deacon at his church. Finally, he is an airline pilot. Regardless of which of his three roles grants him the greatest spiritual insight, his flying career renders him, at the very least, closest to heaven!

In any case, Jerry has compiled the following checklist for believers who are looking to enhance the effectiveness of their prayers.

According to Jerry, this list "is not meant to imply that God is legalistic in His dealings with man. Nor does it imply that God is restricted in what He can do. God is sovereign and He acts according to His will and grace. God often answers our prayers when we don't deserve to be answered and blesses us when we don't deserve to be blessed. The following list does not imply that if something in your life is awry, God can't or won't answer your prayers . . . but it is safe to say that your prayers may well be hindered."

Jerry adds that working prayerfully through this list may help you discover if God is waiting for something to be corrected in your life before He answers your prayer. Take a moment right now to consider some of these items, checking the answers that apply to you.

Do I have unconfessed sin in my life? (Ps. 66:18; 1 John 1:9)	☐ No	☐ Yes
Do I have a clear conscience in asking for this? (1 John 3:21)	☐ Yes	☐ No
Am I listening for God's correction in my life? (Prov. 28:9)	☐ Yes	☐ No
Am I continuing to "practice evil deeds" which I have previously confessed? (John 15:7, 10)	☐ No	☐ Yes
Does God's Word abide in me? (John 15:7)	☐ Yes	☐ No
Do I love those around me? (John 15:7, 10, 12)	☐ Yes	☐ No
Am I praying in the Spirit? (Eph. 6:18; Jude 20)	☐ Yes	☐ No
Have I asked the Holy Spirit to help me with my "weakness" in praying? (Rom. 8:26)		
Am I yielding to the leading of the Holy Spirit? (Rom. 8:26)	☐ Yes	☐ No
Do I always pray "In Jesus' name"? (John 14:13-14; 16:23)	☐ Yes	☐ No
Am I praying in accordance with God's will—both His stated will as revealed in the Bible and His will revealed to us by the Holy Spirit?		

	Yes	No
(1 John 5:14-15)	☐ Yes	☐ No
If I am unsure of God's will in this matter, have I nevertheless committed to God that I want His will, regardless of what it is? (Rom. 8:26-28)	☐ Yes	☐ No
Am I praying with faith? Do I believe that God can and will answer my prayer? (Matt. 21:22; Heb. 11:6)	☐ Yes	☐ No
Have I thanked God for the many things He has already done for me? (Col. 4:2; Phil. 4:6)	☐ Yes	☐ No
Have I forgiven everyone who has sinned against me? (Matt. 6:12, 14, 15; Mark 11:25)	☐ Yes	☐ No
Am I asking with the right motives? (James 4:3; Ps. 37:4)	☐ Yes	☐ No
Is my desire to "seek first the kingdom of God and His righteousness?" (Matt. 6:33; 7:7)	☐ Yes	☐ No
Have I shared my blessings with those who are less fortunate than I am? This can include sharing of my time, money, food, clothing, or shelter. (Prov. 21:13)	☐ Yes	☐ No
If I'm married, is there harmony in my marriage relationship? As a wife, am I submitting to my husband? (1 Peter 3:1) As a husband, am I living with my wife in an understanding way? Am I honoring her? (1 Peter 3:7)	☐ Yes	☐ No

If any of your answers appeared in the right half of the answer column, refer to the Scripture reference given and consider discussing the matter with God in prayer.

It would be nice to think that clearing your heart and soul of all that would hinder your prayers is a one-time exercise. But it's not. So much in the world around us, in our busy lives, and even in our own souls works to gradually reclaim territory we have cleared and staked for Jesus Christ. Keeping the communication lines of prayer open and free from debris requires constant diligence.

Keep this checklist handy. The next time your prayers feel as though they are bouncing off the ceiling—and there *will* be a next time and even many times after that—review these verses which outline the conditions under which your prayers can be effective. Then examine your heart. Confess your shortcomings to the Lord, and He will forgive you (1 John 1:9). Then, and only then, will your prayers begin to wield the kind of impact that can change your life and the lives of those you love best.

Ready, Set, Go!

At this stage in the game, we've examined three ironclad reasons to become parent warriors who are ready and willing to engage in spiritual warfare for their children. We've also reviewed four foundational skills and tools that can help you brandish your prayers more effectively.

And yet prayer—like riding a bike, playing a musical instrument, or even making love—cannot be learned by reading a book, listening to a tape, watching a documentary, talking with someone who prays, or even believing that prayer is a worthwhile endeavor.

Prayer, after all, can only be learned and perfected the old-fashioned way: on our knees.

It's time to pray.

PART THREE:
Adventures in Prayer:
A Twenty-One Day Workbook for Parent Warriors

"Prayer is a powerful thing, for God has bound and tied Himself thereto. None can believe how powerful prayer is, and what it is able to effect, but those who have learned it by experience."

— Martin Luther

You are about to embark on an adventure.

This is because the process of becoming a parent warrior will not only impact your child . . . it will forever change the way you view yourself, your world, and your relationship with God.

In previous chapters we examined our reasons for becoming parent warriors, we talked about the logistics of an effective prayer life centered around our children, and we read stories of men and women who have found solace and solutions through their fervent prayers for the sons and daughters they love.

And yet parent warriorship cannot be mastered by reading a book.

This is why I believe that the following workbook is so important. It is, in fact, the very heart of the bound mass of pages you hold in your hands. This is where the rubber hits the road, where what you "know" becomes what you "believe" in your pursuit of becoming a parent warrior.

This is where it all begins.

Each "day" in the workbook consists of three parts:

ề a devotional

ề a mini-Bible study

ề a prayer journal to assist you in your personal adventures in prayer.

Each day's devotional and Bible study is designed to be completed in about ten minutes — the amount of time you then devote to prayer is up to you.

Among other things, this workbook is designed to help you:

ề establish the pattern of daily prayer for your child — thus, the twenty-one days of this workbook. It is a well-known fact that it takes twenty-one days to change an old habit or to allow a new pattern to take root in your life.

ì establish a better working knowledge of Scriptures that pertain to an effective prayer life.

ì develop the biblically based pattern in your prayers of beginning with praise, then spending a few moments searching your own heart in confession, moving into intercession or "requests," and closing with thanksgiving.

ì practice prayers that are based on God's will as it is revealed in Scripture—each day we will isolate one or more verses that you can "pray" over your children.

ì and finally, develop broader concepts of how to pray for your children. The workbook begins by encouraging you to prepare your heart for effective prayer through confession and worship. It then includes sections on praying for your abilities as a parent, praying for your children's future, praying for protection for your children, and finally, praying for character development as we take a look at eight different traits that God wants to develop in your child.

When I think of praying—and praying scripturally—for my children, I think immediately of the obvious. I know that it is God's will for my children to experience salvation. I know that it is God's will for my children to marry Christian spouses. I know that it is God's will for my children to live godly lives and to resist temptation.

But the Bible is *filled* with verses that tell us how God wants us to live our lives—in *every* area of our lives. There are verses on how we are to communicate, how we are to witness to others, how we are to resolve conflict, all verses that reflect God's will for believers, and are therefore wonderful templates for us to use as we pray for our children.

Using several hundred Bible verses, I have selected eight character traits that God desires to develop in our children. They are:

ì Godly communication
ì A renewed spirit and mind
ì Sexual purity
ì Patience
ì Fear of the Lord
ì Joy

96

≈ Appreciation for the Word of God

≈ Commitment to prayer

In the following workbook each of these traits is examined, along with Bible verses that confirm them.

At the end of the workbook, you will find a Thanksgiving Log. I encourage you to jot down specific requests, and the answers that God provides. It's a wonderful way to remember all the times God has come through, and a way to keep in mind—and continue praying for—those requests that have yet to be answered.

And now, let the adventure begin.

SECTION 1
Preparing Your Heart

Microwave Prayers

"Night and day we pray most earnestly" (1 Thes. 3:10).

We live in the age of phones, FAX, and Federal Express. We drive in the fast lane, carry portable phones into restaurants, and clip pagers to our hips and purses.

To help today's hurried and harried family members, marketers are always coming up with new "time saving" products. Especially when it comes to mealtimes, where we can now feast on a banquet of hasty tasties ranging from microwave brownies to microwave pizza (sort of a fast-food gone faster, I guess). I have yet to see microwave dog food, but nearly everything else in your grocer's aisles can now be purchased in disposable, microwavable packaging. Last week—and I am being serious here because I would never exaggerate something of this significance to the pork industry—I even spotted *microwavable pork rinds*.

If only there was a way to microwave a prayer. Position it in a microwave-safe container, push a button and ZAP . . . I'm out the door and on my way to fulfill my daily agenda.

Unfortunately, prayer can't be rushed. Prayer is, after all, a cornerstone of our relationship with our Creator; it is a conversation of the most intimate sort and requires quantity time as well as quality time.

We expect our prayers to transcend the limitations of earth and our humanity, reaching the heavens and moving the very hand of God. And yet we take this winged and empassioned entreaty called prayer and ask it to take a backseat to the digital clock by our bedside or to the daily planner we carry to and from the office every day.

But there is good news in the form of a potent truth:
We can't outgive God.

I have yet to meet anyone who will admit that time spent daily in prayer is not worth the investment, and/or is not redeemed during the day. Perhaps this is because the moments spent with our Creator serve to "focus" us and enable us to waste less time in the remaining hours of each day. Maybe the eternal perspective we gain when we pray helps us to recognize life's more trivial pursuits and — if not weed them out altogether — at least spend a little less time and energy obsessing over them. Or perhaps it's something as simple and as miraculous as the thought that whatever we give to God He can return to us multiplied — like the fish and the loaves or the jar of oil belonging to the widow and her son.

Whatever the reasons, some of the busiest, most productive Christians are the same men and women who spend consistent and significant time on their knees.

George Washington prayed the first and last hour of virtually every day of his adult life. Martin Luther used to lament that he had so much to do each day that he couldn't afford *not* to begin the day with two hours of prayer. Even Jesus Christ spent whole nights alone in prayer before major decisions throughout His New Testament ministry.

Perhaps, on the other side of eternity, we'll see things in a clearer light and realize that prayer was the single, most effective activity available to us during our years on earth. Maybe, once we calculate all the misdirections we took, mistakes we made, and heartaches we carried by acting *without* praying, we'll recognize that consistent prayer would have saved more time than it took — and changed our lives and our eternity in the process.

So let's take the time — *make* the time — for prayer. Sacrifice a soap opera, if you dare. Get up an hour earlier. Walk the dog. Fast a meal. Take refuge behind a closed door while your kids play video games in the den. Just don't let the days slip away without taking the time to let prayer change your life and the lives of those you love best.

And save the microwave for those pork rinds.

❦ ❦ ❦

99

Bible Study

In Ephesians 6:18 Paul admonishes believers to "pray . . . on all occasions." Again, in 1 Thessalonians 5:17 he tells us to "pray continually." Paul himself prayed night and day, according to his own admission in 1 Thessalonians 3:10. And to Timothy he wrote that he prayed "night and day . . . constantly" (2 Tim. 1:3). By his words—and by his own personal example—Paul put a premium on prayer and encouraged other Christians to do the same.

Exactly how did men and women in biblical days put these kinds of admonitions into practice? When did they pray? Once a week? Once a day? At what hours of the day?

Look up the following Scriptures and see what we are told about the prayer habits of the following Bible personalities:

David prayed . . .
  ☐ Psalm 5:3 *(example: "Morning by morning")*
  ☐ Psalm 88:13 _____
  ☐ Psalm 88:1-2 _____
  ☐ Psalm 55:16-17 _____
Daniel prayed . . .
  ☐ Daniel 6:10 _____
Jesus prayed . . .
  ☐ Luke 6:12 _____
  ☐ Mark 1:35 _____
The apostles prayed . . .
  ☐ Acts 3:1 _____
  ☐ Acts 12:5, 12 _____
  ☐ Acts 16:25 _____

Take a moment and think about a time you can commit to praying specifically for your children. By committing to a specific time—be it daily or weekly—you will have made yourself accountable to God, and to a friend if you so choose.

The downside to making this kind of commitment is that it can give Satan a foothold by blasting you with guilt should you miss one or more of your appointed times with God.

When life gets hectic, it is all the more reason to hold fast to your times of communion and communication with God (especially when you are praying for your children, because when *your* life gets hectic, they feel the tension too). But when you don't—or can't—follow through, don't compound the problem by wallowing in guilt. Guilt is an unpleasant sensation, and it is a fact of human nature that we tend to avoid that which makes us feel guilty. There is nothing Satan would love more than to drive a wedge of guilt between you and God.

So allow the following commitment to serve as a goal and a standard. There will be days you will not meet the standard. So be it. We have been freed from the letter of the law in order to follow the spirit of the law. We are encouraged to "work out our salvation" which takes time and practice. We will make mistakes. It's part of the package. The best we can do is commit our mistakes to the Lord and ask Him to increase our strength and our wisdom so we will be prepared to handle things better in the future.

Consider now what kind of commitment can serve as a standard in your efforts as a parent warrior. In the following statement, please fill in the amount of time you are willing to set aside for prayer, the names of the child(ren) you will be uplifting in prayer, the frequency of this appointment with God, and the time and place you were asked to identify on page 59. My suggestion is that you begin by setting aside some time each day to crack open this workbook, allowing time to conclude with your own prayers for your children. Of course, if you are using this book as a catalyst for a weekly Bible study or prayer time with other parents, the "days" in this workbook can be tackled on a weekly basis, as well.

There will, of course, be many other moments, at many times, when you will feel the need to pray for your children. But allow this committed time to serve as the cornerstone of your prayer life for your children.

At the end of chapter 4 you identified a time and place that would be conducive to prayer. At the end of chapter 5 you also identified a person who could serve as a prayer parrner. Refer now to this information, found on pages 59 and 74, as you complete the following statement:

I commit to spending _____ minutes in prayer on behalf of
(name of child) _____. A workable time
for me to pray is _____. The location at which I will
pray is _____. This will be my time ☐ daily / ☐
weekly with God for the express purpose of protecting, encouraging, and molding my child(ren) through my prayers.

When I choose to pray with a partner, that partner will be
_____. I have contacted this person and
asked him/her to pray with me ☐ on a regular basis / ☐ as
needed.

(Your signature) _____

(Date) _____

Prayer Journal

*As you pray, spend a few moments in praise, confession, petition, and
thanksgiving, incorporating the words of the following Scriptures into
your prayers. When appropriate, personalize each verse with the pronouns "I" or "me" or with the name of your child.*

Regarding praise:

"Shout for joy to the Lord, all the earth. Serve the Lord with
gladness; come before Him with joyful songs. Know that the
Lord is God. It is He who made us, and we are His; we are His
people, the sheep of His pasture" (Ps. 100:1-3).

Regarding confession:

"If we claim to be without sin, we deceive ourselves and the truth
is not in us. If we confess our sins, He is faithful and just and will
forgive us our sins and purify us from all unrighteousness"
(1 John 1:8-9).

Regarding our requests to God:

"If you believe, you will receive whatever you ask for in prayer"
(Matt. 21:22).

How might you personalize this verse to reflect your belief that God will grant you what you ask in regard to your child? Paraphrase the verse in your own words.

_____

_____

Additional topics you may want to discuss with God:
&⬝ Your reasons for wanting to strengthen your prayers for your children.
&⬝ Any concerns or thoughts you might have about your busy schedule and how it might impact your efforts to spend more time in prayer.
&⬝ Ask God to increase your desire to spend time with Him in prayer and to pray diligently for your children.

❦ ❦ ❦

Regarding thanksgiving:

"Enter His gates with thanksgiving and His courts with praise; give thanks to Him and praise His name. For the Lord is good, and His love endures forever; His faithfulness continues through all generations" (Ps. 100:4-5).

❦ ❦ ❦

Space for thoughts, requests, praises, insights, a letter to God, a list of favorite verses on this topic, notes and/or answers to prayer.

_____

_____

_____

_____

_____

_____

_____

_____

_____

❦ ❦ ❦

Preparing Your Heart

DAY 2 — Clean Hearts, Open Ears

"The eyes of the Lord are on the righteous and His ears are attentive to their cry" (Ps. 34:15).

"Grant us grace, Almighty Father, so to pray as to deserve to be heard." —Jane Austen

---

Kaitlyn is a master of many voices. Sometimes, when she's playing with her dolls, she slips into a dainty British accent. Don't ask me where she picked it up—maybe she's been watching too many Haley Mills movies on the Disney Channel.

Then there's her "Texas talk." When we left California two years ago, she was a very articulate four-year-old. Now she slips in and out of an exaggerated Texas accent. It's completely intentional, and so thick that it prompted one of Kaitlyn's friends—Laura Spurlock, who is also six and born and raised in Texas—to ask one day, "Kaitlyn, why are you talking like that?"

Kaitlyn didn't miss a beat. "Ah'm tah-awking Tyexas stiyall."

Laura just said, "Oh," and picked up another Barbie.

I can handle the Queen Mother of England. I can handle Quick Draw McGraw. What I *can't* handle is . . .

. . . The Baby Voice.

When Kaitlyn dons her baby voice, almost everything starts with the letter T and comes out in a whine.

"Maaaama, time tungry."

She thinks she's being cute. Someday some doctor will write a book about this, and maybe I'll understand the psychological significance of this particular self-imposed speech impediment. Until then, all I know is that it drives me nuts.

I've tried reasoning with her, threatening her, bribing her, and yet the Baby Voice always manages to reemerge. There is only one way to kill that voice.

"Kaitlyn, I can't hear you."

"Twhat?"

"I can't hear that voice."

"But time tungry."

Long pause.

"Tye ted time *tungry*."

Longer pause.

"Mama, I'm hungry. Could I have something to eat . . . please?"

According to the Bible, there are certain prayers that God can't hear. We ask. There's a long pause. We ask again. The pause is even longer. God's not listening.

It's not a truth that we enjoy hearing. But it's an important principle that we can't ignore if we want our prayers for our children to have any impact at all.

You'll notice that the prayer journal segment of each day in this workbook begins with a time of confession. As far as I know, God doesn't have an aversion to a six-year-old's interpretation of baby talk. But what He can't tolerate—the one thing that will close His ears to our pleas—is a prayer spoken from a heart harboring sin or rebellion.

I'm sure you've noticed that we are in Day Two of this workbook and we have yet to pray for our children. We aren't going to pray for them today, either. Today we're going to continue to pray for ourselves—for our hearts, that they might be humbled before God so that our prayers will be heard.

If you've flown commercially, you are acquainted with the emergency procedures spiel that flight attendants pantomime at the beginning of every flight: The seat cushions will float . . . emergency exits are here, here, and here . . . the oxygen mask will drop like so. . . .

And if you've flown with a small child, you may have noticed the part about—in case of an emergency—securing *your* oxygen mask *before* you turn to help your children.

Before I became a parent, that seemed like odd advice. But now that I am a mother, I know why I'm asked to secure my oxygen mask before helping my child. I realize that when I am handicapped in any way, I am unable to care for my children. When I am emotionally or spiritually handicapped . . . when I am ill-prepared . . . when I am less than my best . . . when I am hurting or distracted or ineffective in any manner — my children suffer.

Spending time taking care of *your* business with God might seem tangential when, after all, you picked up this book for the purpose of praying for your children.

I assure you that it is not.

Bringing your heart in line with God's . . . making sure your relationship with your Heavenly Father is renewed and healthy . . . confessing anything that might stand in the way of your effective prayers are all foundational to your success as a parent warrior.

After all, we are parents, but we are also children of the Mighty King. And we must approach Him as *His* children before we can approach Him for *our* children.

❧ ❧ ❧

Bible Study

God gives us a series of promises about the conditions that enable Him to hear our prayers for our children:

☐ When we _____, He can hear our prayer. (See Ps. 34:15.)

☐ When we _____, He can hear our prayer. (See Ps. 34:17.)

☐ When we _____, He can hear our prayer. (See John 9:31.)

☐ When we _____, He can hear our prayer. (See Prov. 15:8.)

☐ When we _____, He can hear our prayer. (See Ps. 10:17.)

Tough order, right? If you're like me, you are painfully aware of how often you fall short of these prerequisites for gaining the ear of God. After all, 1 John 1:8, 10, make it clear that *no one* can achieve and maintain rightousness in their own power. Take an-

other look at the verses in 1 John and sum them up in your own
words:

☐ 1 John 1:8 _____

_____

☐ 1 John 1:10 _____

_____

And yet there is a way we *can* approach the throne of God, every
time we pray, in a manner worthy of His attention. Between these
two passages, in 1 John 1:9, lies our hope. Paraphrase this crucial
verse, personalizing it by inserting your name and/or the pronouns "I" and "me" when appropriate:

☐ 1 John 1:9 _____

_____

_____

I like the fact that this potent verse is wedged between two verses
reminding us how truly sinful we are. Accepting God's forgiveness
and cleansing doesn't mean we will never sin again—but in the
very midst of all the mistakes we have made and all the mistakes
we have yet to make, God's forgiveness is ready and waiting only
on our humble confession.

How might you personalize this verse and incorporate this passage into your prayer of confession and submission?

_____

_____

_____

_____

❦ ❦ ❦

Prayer Journal

*As you pray, spend a few moments in praise, confession, petition, and
thanksgiving, incorporating the words of the following Scriptures into
your prayers. When appropriate, personalize each verse with the pronouns "I" or "me" or with the name of your child.*

Regarding praise:

"Who has measured the waters in the hollow of his hand, or with
the breadth of his hand marked off the heavens? Who has held the

dust of the earth in a basket, or weighed the mountains on the scales and the hills in a balance? . . . Lift your eyes and look to the heavens: Who created all these? He who brings out the starry host one by one, and class them each by name. Because of His great power and mighty strength, not one of them is missing" (Isa. 40:12, 26).

Regarding confession:

" 'Even now,' declares the Lord, 'return to Me with all your heart, with fasting and weeping and mourning.' Rend your heart and not your garments. Return to the Lord your God for He is gracious and compassionate, slow to anger and abounding in love and He relents from sending calamity" (Joel 2:12-13).

Regarding our requests to God:

"Search me, O God, and know my heart; test me and know my anxious thoughts. See if there is any offensive way in me, and lead me in the way everlasting" (Ps. 139:23-24).

> *Additional topics you may want to discuss with God:*
> ❧ Ask God to show you areas in your life that are not pleasing to Him.
> ❧ Ask Him to forgive you of anything that is standing in the way of a right relationship with Him.
> ❧ Ask God to allow you to stand before Him, without condemnation, because of Christ's blood that was shed for your sins.

Regarding thanksgiving:

"Give thanks to the Lord, for He is good. His love endures forever. Give thanks to the God of gods. His love endures forever. Give thanks to the Lord of lords; His love endures forever" (Ps. 136:1-3).

Space for thoughts, requests, praises, insights, a letter to God, a list of favorite verses on this topic, notes, and/or answers to prayer.

❧   ❧   ❧

Preparing Your Heart

DAY ~3~ | Heart Worship

"If I had cherished sin in my heart, the Lord would not have listened; but God has surely listened and heard my voice in prayer" (Ps. 66:18-19).

"Be careful to obey all these regulations I am giving you, so that it may always go well with you and your children after you, because you will be doing what is good and right in the eyes of the Lord your God" (Deut. 12:28).

Several months ago I began to use "sitting in the corner" as a technique to discipline my daughter. Until now we've relied on the old standbys: spankings, toy restrictions, and an occasional soapy mouth. But our recent foray into new territories of discipline is memorable.

I'm sure you are aware of the routine, either from your experience as a parent or your days as a rambunctious kid — although I won't ask you to incriminate yourself here. Anyway, I positioned Kaitlyn in a chair facing a blank corner, set the oven timer for fifteen minutes, and asked her to use the time to think about the apology she would need to express to me for the crime that landed her in this predicament: "talking back."

When the timer buzzed, I sat Kaitlyn beside me on the couch and asked if she'd been thinking about an apology.

The beam of accomplishment on her face should have alerted me.

"Oh, yes!" she gushed. "I'm ready!"

And then she launched into the most intriguing apology I've ever received. It was in the form of a poem.

110

A badly rhyming poem, to be sure (she's only six, after all), but still a poem. It went something like: "Mama, I'm very sorry / Please do not be mad at me. / I will never, ever do that again / So don't worry."

Then she glowed up at me. "Wasn't that good?"

I suspected that in the case of this particular apology, form had become more important than function; the method had eclipsed the message. I probed just in case I was wrong: "Kaitlyn, do you remember what you did to get into trouble?"

She looked blank, as if to say, *Mom, get real! That was twenty minutes ago.* Then she shook her head.

Kaitlyn had captured the words, but not the heart of what I was seeking from her. She had missed the point, and managed to miss it broadly even in the midst of an energetic expenditure of time and effort.

She reminds me of a lot of Christians I know.

We all know how to worship, don't we? After all, we worship God for twenty minutes in song on Sunday mornings and — if we're really spiritual — for another twenty minutes on Wednesday or Sunday night.

We might also worship Him when we pray during the week, perhaps even daily as we work our way through the pages of this workbook.

But I wonder if, at times, we are more caught up in form than function; in method than in the message.

Take, for example, the experience of a friend I'll call Tom. Tom was a strong advocate of worship. He knew countless worship hymns; at church he even "subbed in" whenever their music minister had to be away. In his personal life, each time Tom prayed, he began with Bible verses, songs, and words of praise and worship. He even taught a one-day workshop on worship for the men in his church.

In the meantime, Tom worked hard to ignore a few little problems in his life. Tom was harsh and controlling with his children. He fudged a little on his income tax. And whenever he thought he could get away with it, he allowed himself to ogle the ample bosom of the marketing director at his firm.

Tom thought he knew how to worship God in song and in prayer. But he was missing the point.

Henry Morris, in his book *The Genesis Record* (Grand Rapids: Baker/Revell, 1979), writes: "The word 'worship' means simply 'bow down.' Singing hymns and giving testimonies, hearing a preacher and enjoying Christian fellowship is not worshiping, although we speak of such activities as a worship service. To worship God is simply to bow down to His will, recognizing and acknowledging that His will is best. . . . It is then, and only then, that we *worship* God."

Day by day, as you spend time worshiping God through the praise and thanksgiving portions of your prayer journal, remember that true worship is only possible when your heart, as well as your words, bow down to the will of the God we serve. Before you begin to worship God in prayer today, take a look at your heart to determine if there is some area of your life in which you are neglecting, denying, or rationalizing what you know is God's will for you.

When our attitudes and actions are placed firmly in the center of God's will for our lives, then our words of worship will be sweet and satisfying to His ears. We can sing our praises to Him. We can worship in our prayers. We can even write poems — even poems that barely rhyme.

And He will be pleased.

❦ ❦ ❦

Bible Study

The Bible is filled with examples of men and women whose lips paid homage to God while their hearts held out. In the following passage, what ramifications were promised by God when mouths and hearts were not in sync?

☐ Isaiah 29:13-15 _____

_____

Read Acts 4:32-37 and 5:1-11. This story illustrates how severely God views a lack of integrity between our hearts and our lips. According to Acts 5:4, what did this couple do wrong? Was it the fact that they did not donate all the money to the church . . . or did their sin lie elsewhere, and which verse identifies their sin?

_____

If we worship with our mouths, yet our hearts are distracted or harboring sin, can we fool God? Not a chance. Check out and note the similarities in the following verses. What is the point each of these verses makes? What is God intimately acquainted with?
☐ 1 Samuel 16:7 _____
☐ 1 Chronicles 28:9 _____
☐ Jeremiah 17:10 _____

Prayer Journal
As you pray, spend a few moments in praise, confession, petition, and thanksgiving, incorporating the words of the following Scriptures into your prayers. When appropriate, personalize each verse with the pronouns "I" or "me" or with the name of your child.

Regarding praise:
"I will extol the Lord at all times; His praise will always be on my lips. My soul will boast in the Lord; let the afflicted hear and rejoice. Glorify the Lord with me; let us exalt His name together" (Ps. 34:1-3).

Regarding confession:
"Have mercy on me, O God, according to Your unfailing love; according to Your great compassion blot out my transgressions. Wash away all my iniquity and cleanse me from my sin" (Ps. 51:1-3).

Regarding your request:
"Create in me a pure heart, O God, and renew a steadfast spirit within me. Do not cast me from your presence or take your Holy Spirit away from me" (Ps. 51:10-11).

Additional topics you may want to discuss with God:

🖎 That the Holy Spirit would remind you of any forgotten yet unconfessed sins that may be standing in the way of your prayers (see Job 13:23).

🖎 That God's unconditional love for you—in spite of your many imperfections—might be a reminder and a model for you as you strive to love your children unconditionally.

Regarding thanksgiving:

"O Lord, open my lips, and my mouth will declare Your praise. You do not delight in sacrifice, or I would bring it; you do not take pleasure in burnt offerings. The sacrifices of God are a broken spirit; a broken and contrite heart, O God, You will not despise" (Ps. 51:15-17).

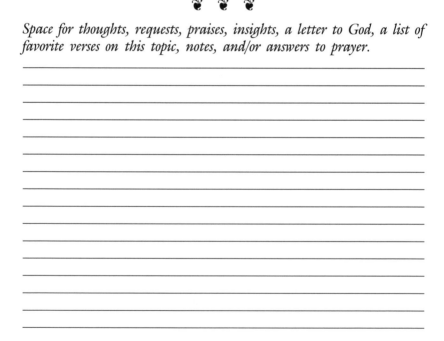

Space for thoughts, requests, praises, insights, a letter to God, a list of favorite verses on this topic, notes, and/or answers to prayer.

Preparing Your Heart

DAY 4 "Dearest Parent Warrior, In Answer to Your Request..."

"They will call on My name and I will answer them" (Zech. 13:9).

It had been a lousy day:

    ... I was under pressure for a writing deadline.

    ... One of our toilets was clogged.

    ... I had hoped to spend the afternoon running errands and had ended up in a traffic jam instead.

    ... The trainee teller at our credit union got confused and had to reprocess my deposit three times.

    ... The lines at the supermarket were serpentine.

I rushed home, sweaty and frustrated, and dropped a bag of groceries on the kitchen table. I grabbed a can of Campbell's cream of mushroom soup for dinner, ran it through the can-opener, and then remembered I'd forgotten to buy milk at the market. Oh, great.

Can the soup idea.

I yanked open the refrigerator door and pulled out a Tupperware tub of leftover baked beans. Cracking the seal, I frowned. Larry's not a picky eater, but even *he* won't eat beans that look like caterpillers.

I fed the garbage disposal and decided to fall back on cuisine as foolproof as it is nutrition free: grilled cheese sandwiches and potato chips. Pulling an unopened bag of chips from the cupboard I gave the cellophane a hardy wrestle.

Nothing happened.

I grunted and doubled the muscle.

The cellophane gave way with a *pop* and ripped wide in my hands. Chips flung sky-high. I was left holding the bag: it was empty.

I groaned. Suddenly I broke loose with a hair-raising scream: "I can't take anymore!"

It was an unorthodox cry for help, to be sure. But Larry heard me and raced to my rescue.

He stood at the door to the kitchen and surveyed the damage: Melting groceries, an opened can of soup, moldy Tupperware, and a quivering wife standing ankle high in a pile of potato chips.

He did what any loving husband would do.

He took a flying leap and landed flat-footed in the pile of chips. Suddenly he was twirling, stomping, dancing, and smashing.

I fumed. I stared. Eventually I had to smile. I finally laughed. And then I danced.

Larry's response wasn't the one I was looking for. But in the end, it probably met my need better than anything else he could have done. I didn't need a clean-up as much as I needed an attitude adjustment: the laughter of the rather unorthodox moment provided just that.

Has God ever stomped on your chips?

Just when we think we know exactly how we want God to answer our prayers, He often responds with an unexpected twist! Sometimes God's response is so different from our expectations that we don't immediately realize that He has, indeed, given us an answer to our prayer! Sometimes we can see right away that God's way of answering our cry for help—even though it was so different than what we had expected—was by far the very best answer! At other times, we might feel disillusioned, disappointed, or even bitter at God's choice of response.

Of course, hindsight has the power to clear up many of these misunderstandings. In time, looking back, I am confident that we will agree with God that His answers to our prayers were the right choices every time.

But until the passage of time grants us the gift of hindsight, how can we tame our disappointment when God answers differently than we expected? How do we increase our faith in God and in His ultimate wisdom and benevolent purpose in our lives?

One of the methods that helps me is to take a big-picture look at the lives of the men and women of the Old and New Testa-

ment. Through the Bible we have access to true-life stories of—
—the prayers of men and women
—how God chose to answer those prayers
—and how, in the end, God's answer proved to be the best possible choice!

As we begin our Bible study for today, let's build our faith by taking a look at the diverse ways God responded to the prayers of godly men and women in biblical days. After all, we're instructed in Hebrews 13:7-8 to "remember your leaders, who spoke the word of God to you. Consider the outcome of their way of life and imitate their faith. Jesus Christ is the same yesterday and today and forever."

The following examples, compiled by Jerry Spurlock, do much to illustrate the fact that God's wisdom is often different than our own when it comes to answering our cries for help! And yet just as He knew what was best for the men and women in biblical days, He remains faithful to us today.

❦ ❦ ❦

Bible Study

As you answer the following questions, keep in mind verses you might want to "pray" over your child. When possible, copy the entire verse from your Bible verbatim or alter it slightly so it includes the name of your child.

In the Old and New Testaments, *God answered the following prayers as they were requested.* What requests were made in the following verses, and how did God answer?

☐ James 5:17
    Request: _____
    Answer: _____
☐ James 5:18
    Request: _____
    Answer: _____
☐ 1 Samuel 1:1-20
    Request: _____
    Answer: _____

The following prayers were answered differently than requested. What were the requests, and how did God choose to answer them?
☐ 2 Corinthians 12:7-9
    Request: _____
    Answer: _____
☐ 2 Samuel 12:15-19
    Request: _____
    Answer: _____
☐ Deuteronomy 3:25-27
    Request: _____
    Answer: _____

The following prayers were not answered in a timely manner — according to the watches and calendars of the men and women in prayer. Summarize each verse or passage in your own words:
☐ Job 30:20 _____
_____
☐ Deuteronomy 1:45-46 _____
_____
☐ Jeremiah 42:1-7 _____
_____

Regardless of how or when God answers our prayers, we can be confident that His answers are best. The following passages assure us of God's wisdom and remind us that we can trust Him always:
☐ Psalm 28:6-7 _____
_____
☐ Isaiah 64:8 _____
_____
☐ Romans 8:28 _____
_____
_____

On another day, you may want to look up additional verses on this subject. Other examples of God's answering prayers *as they were requested* are as follows:

- Hezekiah receives fifteen more years of life (2 Kings 20:1-6).
- Abraham's servant asks for a sign to help him select a wife for Isaac (Gen. 24:14-15).
- Gideon asks for two signs (Jud. 6:36-40).
- Samson prays for God to return his strength (Jud. 16:25-30).
- Elijah brings a child back to life (1 Kings 17:21-22).
- Zechariah prays for a son, and John the Baptist is conceived (Luke 1:13).

Other examples of God's answering prayers *differently than they were requested* are as follows:

- Daniel requested deliverance and receives insight (Dan. 9).
- Jesus prays, "May this cup pass from Me" (Matt. 26:39, 42, 44).
- Solomon asks for wisdom and receives wisdom *and* riches (1 Kings 3:7-14 and 2 Chron. 1:10-12).
- Mary and Martha ask for healing; instead, Lazarus is allowed to die and then is raised from the dead (John 11).

Prayer Journal

As you pray, spend a few moments in praise, confession, petition, and thanksgiving, incorporating the words of the following Scriptures into your prayers. When appropriate, personalize each verse with the pronouns "I" or "me" or with the name of your child.

Regarding praise:

"I love the Lord, for He heard my voice; He heard my cry for mercy. Because He turned His ear to me, I will call on Him as long as I live" (Ps. 116:1-2).

Regarding confession:

"Then I acknowledged my sin to You and did not cover up my iniquity. I said, 'I will confess my transgressions to the Lord'—and You forgave the guilt of my sin" (Ps. 32:5).

Regarding our requests to God:

"Trust in Him at all times, O people; pour out your hearts to Him, for God is our refuge" (Ps. 62:8).

Additional topics you may want to discuss with God:

ᏒᎯ Ask God to multiply your faith and to empower you to trust His answers to your prayers.

ᏒᎯ Ask God to help you recognize His answers when He chooses to repond to your prayers in a manner different than what you expected!

ᏒᎯ Ask God for patience as you wait on His perfect timing.

ᏒᎯ When God's answer to your prayers seems unduly delayed, ask yourself if there is anything in your life that may be hindering your prayers from reaching the ears of God. Review the checklist in chapter 7, asking God to reveal to you anything that is not pleasing to Him.

ᏉᏉᏉ

Regarding thanksgiving:

"Praise our God, O peoples, let the sound of His praise be heard; He has preserved our lives and kept our feet from slipping" (Ps. 66:8-9).

ᏉᏉᏉ

Space for thoughts, requests, praises, insights, a letter to God, a list of favorite verses on this topic, notes, and/or answers to prayer.

_____

_____

_____

_____

_____

_____

_____

_____

_____

ᏉᏉᏉ

SECTION 2

Praying for Your Skills As a Parent

Decisions, Decisions, Decisions...

"If any of you lacks wisdom, he should ask God, who gives generously to all without finding fault, and it will be given to him" (James 1:5).

I believe I need to pray for my children: for their salvation, for their protection, for the development of their characters.

But I also need to pray for the people who influence them daily: their teachers, their peers, their closest friends, and me.

After all, my presence—and my skill or incompetence as a parent—shapes the daily experiences of my children. I help determine their very world. I help shape their personalities, their psyche, their very hearts and souls.

And yet I'm so imperfect!

Have you ever, at the close of a day filled with particularly frustrating family saga, asked yourself which of your parenting mistakes will end up being discussed on a psychologist's couch twenty years from now? Or worse, on the futuristic set of some year-2017 spinoff of Oprah or Geraldo?

I think it is impossible for us to pray effectively for the ones with whom we have been entrusted without praying fervently for our abilities as trustees.

Of course, there are no "Ten Commandments for Parents" that can guide us into knowing what kinds of values, skills, and traits God desires for us to have as moms and dads. Yet the Bible is filled with verses and examples from which we can gleam insight as we journey through our years as parents.

One of the most valuable things for which we can ask—and one of the gifts God is always ready to impart—is wisdom.

121

Today we're going to ask God for wisdom in one of the most critical areas of parenting:

Decision-making.

I don't know about you, but making decisions has never been my strong point. In fact, I've always related to the "double-minded" character that James talks about in the first chapter of his letter: "He who doubts is like a wave of the sea, blown and tossed by the wind" (1:6).

Driven and tossed by a windy sea? I know my decision-making skills have driven some people to want to toss *me* into a windy sea. It took me two months to decide how to answer my husband's marriage proposal and once, in a restaurant, the waitresses changed shifts twice before I actually placed my order.

OK. So maybe they changed shifts once. The point is that it's easy to feel under siege with the number of decisions I have to make as a parent. Whether decisions come easily to you—or whether, like me, you'd just as soon empty the lint trap on your dryer, the sheer quantity of decisions you face as a parent may well leave you feeling overwhelmed. There are, after all, decisions about discipline, schools, playmates, sports, clubs, and music lessons. Decisions about which toys are constructive and which will set my child on a path toward permanent character damage. Decisions about when to let my kids date, when to let them drive, *what* to let them drive.

It would be impossible to pray about every decision that a parent must make in the course of an average day ("Dear Lord, how many 'Weekly Reader' books should we order *this* month?"), but we can certainly pray about the big choices. And as for the smaller, daily decisions, while I might not want to bring each one before the Lord, I can certainly ask God to give me good decision-making skills in general.

James 1:5 says it pretty concisely: "If any of you lacks wisdom, he should ask God, who gives generously to all without finding fault, and it will be given to him."

God wants us to have wisdom—an invaluable asset when it comes to handling decision-making in the '90s. Of course, wisdom might not help me get out of the restaurant any faster, but it'll sure come in handy the next time my kids ask to see a questionable new movie release or want to date someone I don't like.

❦ ❦ ❦

Bible Study

☐ Read Luke 6:12-13. These verses recount four actions on the part of Jesus. Summarize the events in the sequence in which they occurred:

1. _____

2. _____

3. _____

4. _____

The first event discussed reveals something that Jesus did, and the motive behind the action. He went somewhere intending to pray. Did He fulfill His intent? Yes or no? _____ How much time did He invest in fulfilling His intent to pray? _____

Think about praying all night long, alone, on a mountain. What were some of the elements, creatures, and even basic human needs that might have deterred Jesus from fulfilling His intention of praying that night? _____

And yet prayer was of such importance that none of these things stopped Jesus. When you picked up this book—and particularly when you began this workbook—your intention was to spend more time in prayer for your children. How have you been doing in fulfilling that intention? Have you been deterred in meeting your intention? If so, why? _____
How might you reduce these distractions/interruptions/hesitations?

_____

_____

What decision was so important that it drove Jesus to pray all night long on the top of a mountain? _____

_____

If Jesus thought prayer was invaluable before making major decisions in His life, how much more should we depend on prayer prior to *our* decisions as parents! What major decision(s) are you facing as a parent?

_____

Have you prayed about this decision yet? I don't mean a quick word at bedtime or before a meal. Have you set aside a block of time for the express purpose of grappling with God on this particular issue? If not, are you willing to meet with God regarding this issue today?

   _____ Yes   _____ No

If your answer was yes, please do so now.

❦ ❦ ❦

Prayer Journal

As you pray, spend a few moments in praise, confession, petition, and thanksgiving, incorporating the words of the following Scriptures into your prayers. When appropriate, personalize each verse with the pronouns "I" or "me" or with the name of your child.

Regarding praise:

"The Lord foils the plans of the nations; He thwarts the purposes of the peoples. But the plans of the Lord stand firm forever, the purposes of His heart through all generations" (Ps. 33:10-12).

❦ ❦ ❦

Regarding confession:

"Submit to God and be at peace with Him; in this way prosperity will come to you. Accept instruction from His mouth and lay up His words in your heart. If you return to the Almighty, you will be restored" (Job 22:21-23).

❦ ❦ ❦

Regarding our requests to God:

"He will be the sure foundation for your times, a rich store of salvation and wisdom and knowledge; the fear of the Lord is the key to this treasure" (Isa. 33:6).

124

How might you personalize this verse and incorporate it into your prayers for yourself?

_____

_____

_____

Additional topics you may want to discuss with God:

❧ Ask the Holy Spirit to reveal to you times you've made unwise or hasty decisions. If these decisions can be remedied, ask Him how you might go about doing just that. If they are "water under the bridge," ask Him what He wants you to learn from the experience.

❧ Ask God to keep you sensitive to the nudgings of His Holy Spirit so you can be aware of times He wants to direct you even in what might seem like a minor decision.

❧ Ask God to give you, like King Solomon, wisdom beyond your years and experience as a parent.

❧ Ask God to help you become better at observing and listening to your children, so that you might be better prepared to wisely handle the decisions that impact their lives.

❦ ❦ ❦

Regarding thanksgiving:

"I will give thanks to the Lord because of His righteousness and will sing praise to the name of the Lord Most High" (Ps. 7:17).

Space for thoughts, requests, praises, insights, a letter to God, a list of favorite verses on this topic, notes, and/or answers to prayer.

_____

_____

_____

_____

_____

_____

_____

❦ ❦ ❦

125

Praying for Your Skills As a Parent

DAY 6 — Wisdom in Discipline

"[Parents], do not exasperate your children; instead, bring them up in the training and instruction of the Lord" (Eph. 6:4).

Remember Vic and his son, Ronnie? Two years before Vic's amateur "drug raid" and Ronnie's disappearance from home, the family experienced a crisis. Vic was away from home on business when he got a frantic call from his wife.

"Vic, Ronnie just left. I couldn't stop him!" Bonnie screamed into the phone.

Vic, in a motel room several hours from home, clutched the receiver and tried to make sense of Bonnie's hysteria. "Whoa, honey. Slow down. Left? Left where?"

"We've made it *clear* about those boys, Vic. But he's so stubborn! He just won't listen! Here he is, fifteen years old, and running around with . . . with . . . Vic, I don't know what to do with him. I'm at my wit's end. I yelled, he yelled, and then he left. He just ignored me and left. He—"

"He left with Robert?" Vic exploded.

"Robert and that other boy too. You know, the one who was picked up last month for shoplifting!"

"I'm coming home, Bonnie," Vic, turning red, barked into the phone. "When he gets home tonight, lock him in his room if you have to. I'll be home in three hours. *I'll* straighten him out."

Vic drove home in record speed . . . but Ronnie never showed up. By the time the fifteen-year-old dragged in the following day, reeking of alcohol, Vic was beyond control. In the confrontation that followed, he gave in to a rage he'd never vented at any of his

126

children before. He hit Ronnie with his fist.

As Ronnie lay sprawled on the kitchen floor, he glared up at his father with taunting eyes. "Go ahead," he dared, "hit me some more. Beat me up! You weigh 200 pounds. It should be easy for you!"

Looking back, Vic sees only too clearly the mistakes he made that helped push Ronnie farther and farther away.

Of course, there are many ways to exasperate or provoke our children that are not nearly as dramatic as the scene I've just described for you. Unfortunately, provoking our children is easier to do than we might think—especially when it seems as though our children are so experienced at provoking us!

As a pastor, my friend Ron DiGaetano often has the responsibility and privilege of counseling members of his church. Recently he had the chance to meet several times with a single mother and her two teenage daughters. The family had made the appointments to see Ron because of the conflicts they were experiencing at home.

After meeting with the members of the family separately and together, it was easy for Ron to see the root of the problem. Yes, the girls had developed communication patterns that were disrespectful to their mother. Then again, he could see why they had resorted to yelling and shock tactics: their mother never listened to them.

It wasn't that she didn't agree with their opinions—she never *heard* their opinions. She simply never stopped "talking at" her daughters long enough for any real communication to take place. The moment the girls displeased their mother in any way, they were met with a nonstop verbal barrage.

No wonder they rebelled even further.

How we need wisdom when it comes to disciplining and training our children! We spend thirteen years of our lives becoming formally educated with a spectrum of information. Many of us go on to take four more years of formal education designed to help us in our careers. Yet when it comes to raising our children, we're ahead of the crowd if we read a book a year on how to parent.

Thank God that He is willing to help us in this critical endeavor, granting wisdom as we spend time with Him and in His Word!

Bible Study

As you answer the following questions, keep in mind verses you might want to "pray" over your child. When possible, copy the entire verse from your Bible verbatim or altered slightly so it includes the name of your child.

☐ Read Ephesians 6:4. This verse gives two alternatives to provoking your children to wrath. What are they?
1. _____
2. _____

What does it mean to "admonish" your child in the Lord? How does our Heavenly Father admonish us?

☐ Look up 1 Corinthians 4:14. Summarize the verse below, underlining the emotion that admonition is not supposed to evoke.

_____

_____

We know from the way God admonished the Corinthian church through the Apostle Paul that God does not intend for us to feel shame. One dictionary defined shame as a "humilating dishonor." Discipline directs the actions; shame attacks the person. Are there things we say to our children that can cause shame? Examples might be: "You'll never amount to much if you continue acting like that." . . . "Why can't you be more like your sister?" . . . "I should have known you'd find a way to mess up again." . . . "You are such a disappointment to your mother and me."

☐ Acts 20:31 gives another example of an admonition by Paul. Notice that this time he admonished with _____.

☐ Colossians 1:28 describes admonishment—or warning—for what purpose: _____ and aided by what: _____.

☐ Finally Colossians 3:16 encourages believers to admonish one another using the following unlikely methods: _____, _____, and _____. We are also encouraged to admonish one another while doing what: _____ _____.

One dictionary defines "admonish" in the following manner: "to reprove mildly." In the space below, write your own definition of admonish, using key words from the Scriptures above:
ad•mon•ish (ad-'män-ish):

_____
_____
_____
_____
_____
_____

Can you "admonish your children in the Lord"? How might the above definition of admonish alter the way you have tried to discipline in the past?

_____
_____
_____

In Philippians 1:9, Paul's prayer for the believers in Philippi was that their love would coexist with knowledge and good judgment. Ask God to multiply these three dynamics in your life. Finally, read Solomon's prayer for wisdom in 1 Kings 3:7-9. What was his request? _____

_____

What a powerful prayer for us to apply to our lives as we seek to judge, discern, and discipline the children God has charged to our care! How might you personalize this passage and "pray" it for your own life?

_____
_____
_____
_____
_____
_____

_____
_____
_____

Prayer Journal

As you pray, spend a few moments in praise, confession, petition, and thanksgiving, incorporating the words of the following Scriptures into your prayers. When appropriate, personalize each verse with the pronouns "I" or "me" or with the name of your child.

Regarding praise:

"I will give You thanks, for You answered me; You have become my salvation" (Ps. 118:21).

Regarding confession:

"Do not be wise in your own eyes; fear the Lord and shun evil. This will bring health to your body and nourishment to your bones. . . . My son, do not despise the Lord's discipline and do not resent His rebuke, because the Lord disciplines those He loves, as a father the son He delights in" (Prov. 3:7-8, 11-12).

Regarding our requests to God:

"My son, *if* you accept My words and store up My commands within you, turning your ear to wisdom and applying your heart to understanding, and *if* you call out for insight and cry aloud for understanding, and *if* you look for it as for silver and search for it as for hidden treasure, *then* you will understand the fear of the Lord and find the knowledge of God. For the Lord gives wisdom, and from His mouth come knowledge and understanding" (Prov. 2:1-6, italics added). How might you personalize this passage and "pray" these verses for your own life?

_____
_____
_____

_____

_____

_____

_____

Additional topics you may want to discuss with God:

🍎 In this passage, note the list of conditions set apart by the word "if." Meet these conditions and God will give you wisdom, knowledge, discretion, and understanding. Ask God to help you meet these conditions by enabling you to:

— accept His words
— cherish His commandments
— listen closely and recognize wisdom when you hear it
— desire greater understanding
— pray for insight and understanding
— value wisdom more than money or material things

🍎 You may also want to pray this same verse for your child. Ask God to develop character traits and desires in your child that will help her to meet the conditions that will allow her to receive wisdom, knowledge, discretion, and understanding too!

🍎　🍎　🍎

Regarding thanksgiving:

"May my lips overflow with praise, for You teach me Your decrees. . . . Let me live that I may praise You, and may Your laws sustain me" (Ps. 119:171, 175).

As you begin to meet the conditions set forth in Proverbs 2:1-6, you can rest assured that God will begin to multiply your wisdom, knowledge, and understanding. He will also give you the blessings mentioned in Proverbs 2:7-9. Begin now, in faith, to thank God for responding to your efforts by giving you:

— a healthy fear of the Lord
— wisdom
— knowledge and understanding
— victory
— Himself as a shield

—safety and protection as you journey through life
—wisdom, knowledge, discretion, and understanding when it comes to knowing what is right and just and fair . . . especially in matters relating to the training and disciplining of your child!

🍎　🍎　🍎

Space for thoughts, requests, praises, insights, a letter to God, a list of favorite verses on this topic, notes, and/or answers to prayer.

\
\
\
\
\
\
\
\
\
\
\
\
\
\
\
\
\
\
\
\
\
\
\
\
\
\
\
\
\
\

🍎　🍎　🍎

Praying for Your Skills As a Parent

DAY 7 — Praying Parents Make Better Parents (Part I)

"Be devoted to one another in brotherly love. Honor one another above yourselves. Never be lacking in zeal, but keep your spiritual fervor, serving the Lord. Be joyful in hope, patient in affliction, faithful in prayer" (Rom. 12:10-12).

The above verse was written to apply to my relationships with the friends, fellow believers, and strangers with whom I come into contact. There is little doubt that the eight exhortations Paul gives in this letter, if put into practice, would have the power to enhance virtually any relationship.

But do I dare apply this verse to my relationship with my children? Why is it that my best social behavior, gentlest manners, and kindest words are on display during Bible study but not at home where *my* life is the textbook under avid study by some of God's smallest students?

Being affectionate comes fairly easy. But dare I give honor to my six-year-old by finding appropriate times to give preference to some of her opinions and desires? How fervent is my spirit at the thought of another morning of "Sesame Street" with my two-year-old?

How much "patience in affliction" do I model for a fifteen-year-old? (Granted, that fifteen-year-old may *be* my affliction. . . .)

Neil Anderson and Steve Russo, in their book *The Seduction of Our Children* (Eugene, Ore.: Harvest House, 1991) touch on these important concepts when they advise parents regarding the importance of showing respect to their children: "[Children] are little adults created in the image of God. Talk to them with the same sense of respect you would extend to an adult."

133

Sounds great. But if you're like me, you're realizing that words like these are easier said than done.

I really appreciate the exhortation found in Romans 12:10-12. The list of attitudes and behaviors are admirable and desirable—and, if applied in my home, would certainly help me show respect to my children and improve my skill as a parent! But the most significant of the bunch—perhaps even the single action that makes all the first seven even remotely possible—are the final words:

"be . . . faithful in prayer."

Here, then, is the key. Prayer is the very tool that can enable us to practice godly characterics in our relationships, especially in our relationships with our children—the most exasperating and yet most impressionable of any beings with whom we have the profound privilege of interacting.

Perhaps the entire concept is best summed up by my friend Diane Watson. The mother of two, she made the following observation at the end of a rather long day:

"When I've been praying for my kids, I don't yell at them so much." Then, in a moment of candor she admitted: "I guess I should start praying again!"

For me, the prayer is a simple one. Yet, oh, how necessary. And how easily forgotten!

God, help me to let an attitude of prayer cloak the words and deeds I direct toward the most impressionable members of my household: my children. Familiarity breeds contempt, or so the adage goes.

But even old adages must bow to You and to Your hand in yielded hearts. In my home, Lord, let our familiarity with one another foster holiness. And encouragement. And kindness. And God, let it begin with me.

❦ ❦ ❦

Bible Study

As you answer the following questions, keep in mind verses you might want to "pray" over your child. When possible, copy the entire verse from your Bible verbatim or alter it slightly so it includes the name of your child.

Pop quiz! Take a moment to briefly examine your relationship with your children. Does your behavior exemplify godly traits and characteristics? Would you treat a member of your church in the manner you treat your children? Do your children see God's love reflected in your attitude and behavior toward them? The following questions and verses may help you take a fresh look at your relationship with your children:

Does your anger frequently control your relationship with your children? Read the following verses and summarize God's thoughts regarding your anger:

☐ Proverbs 14:17 _____
Can you think of a time your swift anger has caused you to act toward your child in a manner you later regretted? Think about that incident. How might you have acted less foolishly or destructively? _____

☐ Proverbs 15:18 _____
Has an angry response on your part ever provoked an already tense relationship with your child? Ponder that incident for a moment. Could a different response have promoted healing rather than strife? If so, how? _____
_____

☐ Proverbs 22:24-25 _____
How might this verse apply to the above example set by an angry parent? What danger does it pose to the child who lives in this kind of environment? _____
_____

☐ Read James 1:19. How might you personalize this verse and incorporate it into your prayers for yourself?
_____
_____
_____
_____

Do you need more patience in your parenting? God is not silent on the importance of practicing patience in our lives. What do the following verses teach us about patience?

☐ 1 Thessalonians 5:14 ⎯⎯⎯⎯⎯⎯⎯⎯⎯⎯⎯⎯

⎯⎯⎯⎯⎯⎯⎯⎯⎯⎯⎯⎯⎯⎯⎯⎯⎯⎯⎯⎯⎯⎯⎯⎯⎯

☐ Ecclesiastes 7:8-9 ⎯⎯⎯⎯⎯⎯⎯⎯⎯⎯⎯⎯⎯

How might you incorporate this verse into your prayers for yourself? ⎯⎯⎯⎯⎯⎯⎯⎯⎯⎯⎯⎯⎯⎯⎯⎯⎯⎯⎯⎯⎯⎯

☐ James 1:3-4 ⎯⎯⎯⎯⎯⎯⎯⎯⎯⎯⎯⎯⎯⎯⎯⎯⎯

Have you ever considered the many exhausting trials of parenting
as resources for God to use in the development and sharpening of
godly characteristics in your life? What better place to let "patience
have her perfect work" than in your own home and in your relationship with the ones you love best!

*Are you a happy parent? Or is joy missing from your countenance as
you dutifully master the many responsibilities in your busy life? Do you
realize it's God's will for you to experience joy?* Summarize the
following:
☐ Psalm 28:7: ⎯⎯⎯⎯⎯⎯⎯⎯⎯⎯⎯⎯⎯⎯⎯⎯

⎯⎯⎯⎯⎯⎯⎯⎯⎯⎯⎯⎯⎯⎯⎯⎯⎯⎯⎯⎯⎯⎯⎯⎯⎯

☐ Galatians 5:22 ⎯⎯⎯⎯⎯⎯⎯⎯⎯⎯⎯⎯⎯⎯⎯
☐ Philippians 4:4 ⎯⎯⎯⎯⎯⎯⎯⎯⎯⎯⎯⎯⎯⎯⎯

⎯⎯⎯⎯⎯⎯⎯⎯⎯⎯⎯⎯⎯⎯⎯⎯⎯⎯⎯⎯⎯⎯⎯⎯⎯⎯

⎯⎯⎯⎯⎯⎯⎯⎯⎯⎯⎯⎯⎯⎯⎯⎯⎯⎯⎯⎯⎯⎯⎯⎯⎯⎯

⎯⎯⎯⎯⎯⎯⎯⎯⎯⎯⎯⎯⎯⎯⎯⎯⎯⎯⎯⎯⎯⎯⎯⎯⎯⎯

⎯⎯⎯⎯⎯⎯⎯⎯⎯⎯⎯⎯⎯⎯⎯⎯⎯⎯⎯⎯⎯⎯⎯⎯⎯⎯

⎯⎯⎯⎯⎯⎯⎯⎯⎯⎯⎯⎯⎯⎯⎯⎯⎯⎯⎯⎯⎯⎯⎯⎯⎯⎯

⎯⎯⎯⎯⎯⎯⎯⎯⎯⎯⎯⎯⎯⎯⎯⎯⎯⎯⎯⎯⎯⎯⎯⎯⎯⎯

The above verses express some of God's "blueprints" for our
relationships with those He has placed in our lives. God is hon-
ored when we exercise godly traits in our relationships—and our
relationships with our children are no exception!

Prayer Journal

As you pray, spend a few moments in praise, confession, petition, and thanksgiving, incorporating the words of the following Scriptures into your prayers. When appropriate, personalize each verse with the pronouns "I" or "me" or with the name of your child.

Regarding praise:

"I will praise the Lord, who counsels me; even at night my heart instructs me. I have set the Lord always before me. Because He is at my right hand, I will not be shaken" (Ps. 16:7-8).

Regarding confession:

"How many wrongs and sins have I committed? Show me my offense and my sin" (Job 13:23).

Regarding our requests to God:

Select one of the verses from the Bible study and use it as a basis for your intercession regarding your relationship with your child.

Which verse did you select? _____
If you haven't already answered this question in the previous section, how might you pray this verse for your relationship with your child? _____
_____
_____
_____

Additional topics you may want to discuss with God:
&ash; Ask God to show you how to incorporate godly traits and characteristics into your relationship with your child.
&ash; We are to model God's love to everyone—and particularly to the children who watch us like hawks and model all that we do! Ask God to develop your ability to be a godly example for your child.
&ash; Do you doubt your ability to consistently reflect godly traits

in your relationship with your children? If you fear you can't do it on your own, you are wiser than many! Admit to God how much you need His help in this area. You *can't* do it alone. Only through prayer and submission to the directives of the Holy Spirit can you begin to let godly characteristics override the anger, frustrations, impatience, and exhaustion that are normal by-products of almost any relationship—and particularly the relationship between parents and their children!

❧ ❧ ❧

Regarding thanksgiving:

"It is good to praise the Lord and make music to Your name, O Most High, to proclaim Your love in the morning and Your faithfulness at night, to the music of the ten-stringed lyre and the melody of the harp. For You make me glad by Your deeds, O Lord; I sing for joy at the works of Your hands. How great are Your works, O Lord, how profound Your thoughts!" (Ps. 92:1-5)

❧ ❧ ❧

Space for thoughts, requests, praises, insights, a letter to God, a list of favorite verses on this topic, notes, and/or answers to prayer.

❧ ❧ ❧

Praying for Your Skills As a Parent

DAY 8 Praying Parents Make Better Parents (Part II)

"He will turn the hearts of the fathers to their children, and the hearts of the children to their fathers; or else I will come and strike the land with a curse" (Mal. 3:8).

Yesterday we looked at reducing anger and increasing our patience and joy as part of maintaining and modeling a godly relationship with our children.

But modeling godly characteristics in our relationships with our children requires something else, as well. And this one may be harder to come by.

It's the T word.

That's right—*time.*

You're probably thinking, *Oh, great! It's not enough that this woman demands I set aside some time to pray! Now she's telling me to look at how much time I spend with my children too! What does she think I'm made of . . . clock springs? Just where is all this extra time supposed to come from?*

And yet—let's be honest now—we all know that the quality-time myth has gone belly-up. Our children, darn it all, simply refuse to be scheduled. I can't understand it, can you?

Erma Bombeck, in her book *Motherhood, the Second Oldest Profession* takes a side-splitting and heart-rendering look at the myth of quality time. In three perfect pages, she paints a picture of the world's most efficient and productive mother: Among other things, "Sharon" found time to paint the inside of her garbage cans with enamel, grow her own vegetables, launder aluminum foil and use it again, write her congressman, pack nutritious lunches, save antifreeze from year to year, build a bed out of scraps left over from the patio, put a basketball "hoop" over the clothes hamper to encourage good habits, started seedlings in a toilet paper spindle, and insulated her home with empty egg cartons.

Bombeck goes on to list the many people who said Sharon was Super Mom. Her husband said it. Her kids' teachers said it. Her best friend said it. Her gynecologist said it. Her butcher said it. Her tennis partner said it. Her children . . .

"Her children never said it," Erma concluded:

"They spent a lot of time with Rick's mother, who was always home and who ate cookies out of a box and played poker with them."

I let my neighbor read this chapter from Erma's book. She's read it several times, in fact, and says she has yet to finish it with a dry eye. It's so easy—especially, I believe, for Christians—to "be there" for everyone else in the whole world, while our children get the leftovers.

And even when we think we're spending time . . . are we *really*?

I struggle with this one. Oh, sure. I spend lots of time with my daughter—but it's so often on *my* terms. "Come on, Kaitlyn, we're going to the store. What? You want me to play Barbies with you? Oh, no, honey. But we'll be together anyway—in the car. Hurry now, don't make Mama late! What? *After* the store? Well, actually, afterward we've got to mail this package to Mama's publisher. And then we'll come home and make dinner. Huh? Wash the vegetables? Well, no, you can't wash the vegetables—you take too long. When you're older. But tonight you can watch cartoons while I cook."

Why is it, when I tuck Kaitlyn into bed at night after a day like the one I've just described, *I* feel like we've been together all day long—and *she's* wondering why I don't have time for her?

Time and time throughout the Old and New Testament parents are instructed to teach their children. Yet teaching takes time. It can't be hurried, compacted, or fast-forwarded. This kind of teaching can't be delegated to school teachers, coaches, or baby-sitters, nor relegated to conveniently scheduled snippets of time.

I think Malachi 4:6 says a mouthful, don't you? "He will turn the hearts of the fathers to their children, and the hearts of the children to their fathers; or else I will come and strike the land with a curse." I think, in fact, it describes pretty poignantly what we are witnessing in the lives of our nation's young people today. I don't think, in fact, that "curse" is too strong of a word to describe the current statistics on substance abuse, sexual activity, sexually transmitted diseases, suicide, and sexual abuse among the children of the preoccupied men and women who make up our nation today.

Parenting demands our time. And yet there is no investment on earth that reaps better rewards. As we submit our requests that God will make us better parents, let's not forget to submit our "to-do lists" and Daytimers as well.

❧ ❧ ❧

Bible Study

As you answer the following questions, keep in mind verses you might want to "pray" over your child. When possible, copy the entire verse from your Bible verbatim or alter it slightly so it includes the name of your child.

Do the daily rigors of career, finances, ministry, marriage, and family leave you too drained in the evening to make much of an investment in the lives of your children?

☐ What does 1 Timothy 5:8 tell us about the priority of the members of your family? _____

☐ Read Deuteronomy 6:5-7. What kind of investment are parents instructed to make in the lives of their children? Name the four times or events that are specifically mentioned in these verses as prime opportunities for parents to instill spiritual insights into their children:

1. _____

Are there frequent opportunities in your home for you to engage in this activity with your child? If so, when was the last time you sat and visited with your child about spiritual truths or about life in general — perhaps as it related to school or work, friends, values, problems, disappointments, dreams, goals, or relationships — or even just spent the time joking around? Describe the specific day and the nature of your conversation: _____

_____

If this is difficult to do, pinpoint a day or a time of day you might be able to enjoy some quiet time sitting in your home and visiting with your child:

_____

Check this box after you have invested this time with your son or daughter: ☐

2. _____ _____

When was the last time you engaged in this activity with your child? Describe the specific day and the nature of your conversation: _____

_____

If this is difficult to do, pinpoint a day or a time of day you might be able to enjoy walking and talking with your child: _____

_____

Check this box after you have invested this time with your son or daughter: ☐

3. _____ _____

When was the last time you spent some quality before-bedtime moments with your child? Sorry, baths and face-washings and bedtime drinks don't count for this particular exercise! Also, try not to use your child's age as an excuse: A friend of mine spends a half-hour each evening reading to her eleven-year-old son. What about you? Describe the specific day and the nature of your last meaningful bedtime exchange: _____

_____

If this is difficult to do, pinpoint a day you might be able to enjoy some quiet before-bed moments with your child: _____

_____

Check this box after you have invested this time with your child: ☐

4. _____

When was the last time you began the day with some *quality* time together? If your household is as crazy as mine, you might be tempted to answer, "When she was in the womb." Then again, you might be more than able to describe the specific day and nature of recent A.M. quality time spent with your child: _____

_____

If not, pinpoint a morning you can set the alarm earlier and begin your day by investing in your relationship with your child: ____

_____

Check this box after you have invested this time with your son or daughter: ☐

Prayer Journal

As you pray, spend a few moments in praise, confession, petition, and thanksgiving, incorporating the words of the following Scriptures into your prayers. When appropriate, personalize each verse with the pronouns "I" or "me" or with the name of your child.

Regarding praise:
"My heart is steadfast, O God; I will sing and make music with all my soul. Awake, harp and lyre! I will awaken the dawn. I will praise You, O Lord, among the nations; I will sing of You among the peoples" (Ps. 108:1-3).

Regarding confession:
"Return . . . to the Lord your God. Your sins have been your downfall! Take words with you and return to the Lord. Say to Him: 'Forgive all our sins and receive us graciously, that we may offer the fruit of our lips' " (Hosea 14:1-2).

Regarding our requests to God:
"Love the Lord your God with all your heart and with all your soul and with all your strength. These commandments that I give

you today are to be upon your hearts. Impress them on your children. Talk about them when you sit at home and when you walk along the road, when you lie down and when you get up" (Deut. 6:5-7).

How might you personalize this passage and incorporate it into your prayers for your relationship with your child?

_____

_____

_____

Additional topics you may want to discuss with God:

&. Ask God to open your eyes to opportunities to teach His precepts and His principles to your child.

&. Ask God to turn your heart toward your child, and the heart of your child toward you.

&. Ask God to help you spend time with your child — on your child's terms, not yours.

Regarding thanksgiving:

"Give thanks to the Lord, for He is good; His love endures forever" (Ps. 107:1).

Space for thoughts, requests, praises, insights, a letter to God, a list of favorite verses on this topic, notes, and/or answers to prayer.

_____

_____

_____

_____

_____

_____

_____

_____

_____

SECTION 3

Praying for Your Child's Future

In Search of a Godly Spouse

"Do not be yoked together with unbelievers. For what do righteousness and wickedness have in common? Or what fellowship can light have with darkness?" (2 Cor. 6:14)

Three weeks before her third birthday, Kaitlyn came home from preschool and announced she had a "boyfriend." Actually, he was an older man—someone in the four-year-olds' class.

Two days later my daughter came home in tears. Right there, right at "their" spot in the sandbox, Frankie had told her he didn't want to be her boyfriend anymore. There was (sob) another woman.

Kaitlyn took it hard.

I took it even harder.

I realized just how hard I was taking it the next day as I faced the cashier at Target and handed her $60 for a stack of high-fashion toddler clothes. I guess I figured that, while I couldn't help Frankie make the right dating decisions, I sure could help him regret making the wrong one.

However, before I could teach Kaitlyn to say, "Frankie, eat your heart out" with just the right flair, she came home from preschool with good news. She and Frankie were together again.

When I asked about the other girl, Kaitlyn beamed: "She's his girlfriend too! We're *both* his girlfriends!"

Quite a boy, that Frankie.

I started to explain the concept of two-timing, but decided against it. My daughter was growing up too fast already. I wanted to leave something for the kindergarten years. But I had to wonder how I'm going to make it through the next fifteen or twenty

145

years. After all, I barely made it through my *own* dating years. Now I've got to survive Kaitlyn's too?

The road that leads to the selection of a lifetime partner has never been smooth. It wasn't for me. I think I can assume that it wasn't for you, either. And I'm confident that our children will have their share of bumps and potholes and detours as well. In light of this fact, is it ever too soon to begin praying for the man or woman who will become the helpmate of your child?

Friends Ron and Christine DiGaetano began praying for the future spouse of their daughter when Sarah was still in the womb.

Last year, at the request of my sister Michelle, my mother added fasting to her prayers for Michelle's future spouse. (Last month, I was able to attend Michelle's wedding in California — her new husband, Russ, is a godly man whose sparkling personality seems like a custom-fit for my lovable and sometimes-quirky sister!)

I was in my early teens when my mother and I started praying for the man who would become my husband. I believe that those prayers reached across the miles and somehow, in some way, impacted the life of a high school kid named Larry who was living in Anderson, Indiana.

But those prayers also had an impact closer to home. They did something for me, as my folks and I walked the precarious line through my dating years. I believe my parents' prayers held up a standard — they reminded me that I belonged to God, that my future husband belonged to God, and that our life together was in God's hands. That standard saw me through rebellious years, through heartaches, through lonely weekends, through gut-churning first dates and even through the heady discovery of the sexual chemistry that can ignite between a young man and woman.

Kaitlyn is in kindergarten now. Luckily, we have yet to encounter crisis number two in *her* dating saga. But I realize that it's just a matter of time. And maybe that thought isn't quite as scary as it used to be.

How will I survive her dating years? Perhaps the same way my parents survived mine. On my knees.

Bible Study

As you answer the following questions, keep in mind verses you might want to "pray" over your child. When possible, copy the entire verse from your Bible verbatim or alter it slightly so it includes the name of your child.

Praying that our children will marry believers is an important part of parent warriorship. As we pray for the salvation of our future sons and daughters-in-law, let's also remember to pray for some additional characteristics that the Bible identifies.

Characteristcs of a godly man:

What do the following verses tell us about the kind of men who would be desirable husbands for our daughters? If you don't have a daughter, work through the verses anyway. Part of praying for a godly spouse for your child is asking God to prepare your child to *be* a godly partner, as well. If you are the parent of one or more boys, use these verses for inspiration as you ask God to prepare your son for his future role as a godly man, husband, and father.

☐ Proverbs 19:22 _____

☐ 1 Timothy 6:11 _____

☐ 1 Peter 3:7 _____

☐ Ephesians 5:25, 28-30 _____

Characteristics of a godly woman:

What do the following verses tell us about the kind of women who would be desirable wives for our sons? If you do not have a son and therefore will not be in need of a daughter-in-law, ask God to develop these traits in your daughter(s).

☐ Proverbs 12:4 _____

☐ Ephesians 5:33 _____

Take a moment to read the well-known passage found in Proverbs 31:10-31, regarding the makings of a virtuous woman. Find and note the verse or verses that describe the following characteristics:

Trustworthy: _____

Creative: _____

Hardworking: _____

Takes care of her health: _____

Uses financial common sense: _____

Good steward of her money: _____

Compassionate: _____

Is a good parent: _____

A believer: _____

Optimistic: _____

Prayer Journal

As you pray, spend a few moments in praise, confession, petition, and thanksgiving, incorporating the words of the following Scriptures into your prayers. When appropriate, personalize each verse with the pronouns "I" or "me" or with the name of your child.

Regarding praise:

"My heart rejoices in the Lord; in the Lord my horn is lifted high. My mouth boasts over my enemies, for I delight in Your deliverance" (Hannah's prayer of praise after the dedication of the son she prayed earnestly to conceive.) (1 Sam. 2:1-2).

Regarding confession:

"Blessed is he whose transgressions are forgiven, whose sins are covered. Blessed is the man whose sin the Lord does not count against him and in whose spirit is no deceit" (Ps. 32:1-2).

Regarding our requests to God:

Select a verse from today's Bible study and use it as a basis for your intercession regarding your child's selection of a godly spouse.

Which verse did you select? _____
How might you pray this verse for your child or for your child's future spouse?

_____
_____
_____

Additional topics you may want to discuss with God:
❧ That He might help your child to resist sexual temptation in the years before your child selects and marries a godly spouse (see 2 Tim. 2:22).

❧ That you and your spouse might, in your marriage and in your interactions with one another, serve as godly role models for your children. (Even Paul served as a role model for his spiritual children. See Phil. 4:9.)

❦ ❦ ❦

Regarding thanksgiving:
"And whatever you do, whether in word or deed, do it all in the name of the Lord Jesus, giving thanks to God the Father through Him" (Col. 3:17).

❦ ❦ ❦

Space for thoughts, requests, praises, insights, a letter to God, a list of favorite verses on this topic, notes, and/or answers to prayer.

_____
_____
_____
_____
_____
_____
_____
_____
_____
_____

❦ ❦ ❦

Praying for Your Child's Future

Spiritual Gifts and Ministry

"May Your deeds be shown to Your servants, Your splendor to their children. May the favor of the Lord our God rest upon us; establish the work of our hands for us — yes, establish the work of our hands" (Ps. 90:16-17).

Yesterday Kaitlyn came home from kindergarten with a sheaf of papers stapled together. The cover of her "book" was entitled *My Three Wishes*. Inside, there were three blank pages.

I am a college graduate — I catch on quickly to these kinds of things. I asked her to make three "just for fun" wishes.

As I began looking for crayons so we could attempt to draw some colorful but vague represention of these forthcoming wishes, Kaitlyn pondered the question with a weighty expression on her tiny face. She then began a confident recital of her answers. Amazingly enough, Barbies and Showbiz Pizza weren't mentioned in any of them.

"First, I would wish that my grandparents and cousins could live here in Texas with us," she explained with a very serious expression.

I nodded.

"Then, I would wish that everybody in the whole world would know God."

"OK. Next?"

"Then I would wish that everybody everywhere would get everything they want . . . and be happy . . . and love Jesus."

Two out of three wishes had something to do with God — evangelism, even. Granted, wish number three was something of a combo special, alluding to wealth and happiness and spiritual renewal as well. But still. Two out of three ain't bad.

I believe that as parents, one of our most important tasks is to prepare our children for mission and ministry. God calls each one of us to glorify Him and serve Him. We are each called to minister—whether we do it from a pulpit, through the written word, on our lunch break at work, in the nursery on Sunday mornings, or over coffee friend to friend. God has a plan for each of our lives—and for the lives of each of our children—and part of our responsibility as mothers and fathers is to help our children become sensitive to the Holy Spirit so He can bring that plan to fruition in their lives.

What will Kaitlyn do when she grows up? How will she serve God? I have no idea. But I can begin today exposing her to the variety of ways God chooses to work through His children. I can let her see ways in which I manage to minister to the people around me, and how I allow myself to receive the ministering touch of those people God brings into my path. I can begin impressing on her—now—the fact that her life is not her own, but belongs to God.

And, above all, I can pray.

❧ ❧ ❧

Bible Study

As you answer the following questions, keep in mind verses you might want to "pray" over your child. When possible, copy the entire verse from your Bible verbatim or alter it slightly so it includes the name of your child.

In Psalm 90:16-17, David asks God to "establish the work" of his hands. The following verses show the diversity in "God's work." Write the calling or callings mentioned in each verse:
- ☐ 1 Corinthians 3:6-7 _____
- ☐ 1 Corinthians 3:10 _____
- ☐ 1 Corinthians 12:8 _____
- ☐ 1 Corinthians 12:9 _____
- ☐ 1 Corinthians 12:10 _____
- ☐ 1 Corinthians 12:28 _____

What should our attitude be toward people whose gifts are different than ours? _____
  ☐ 1 Corinthians 12:21 _____
  ☐ 1 Corinthians 12:25-26 _____

Based on 1 Corinthians 12:4-6, 18, who determines our gifts and the kind of work to which we are called? _____

Tom and Junine are very special friends of ours. They were all set to enter the mission field as a couple, following in the footsteps of Tom's parents who, for years, had had an effective ministry in South America. When illness caused Tom and Junine to cancel their plans abroad, they began praying for God's direction. Before long, the couple became focused on ministry stateside as Tom assumed the youth pastorate of our church. God is using Tom and Junine—yet Tom's parents experienced shattering disappointment when Tom and his wife did not use their gifts the way his parents had envisioned.

Perhaps we as parents need to remember that God determines the gifts and ministry of our children—our job is to keep ourselves sensitive to the leading of the Holy Spirit as we raise our children, and teach our children to be sensitive as the Holy Spirit directs their lives.

It might also be necessary to ask God to prepare *us* for whatever it is He has called each of our children to do for Him in their adult lives. After all, there's nothing we would like more, as parents, than for our children to lead happy, safe, and protected lives. Unfortunately, when we serve God with all our hearts and souls—which is *also* something we would like to see in the lives of our children—life can become anything but safe and protected.

John 15:18-20 reminds us of the cost that can be incurred when we submit ourselves to God and allow Him to "establish the work of our hands" (Ps. 90:17)—and the work of our children's hands. According to the verse, what might your children experience when they become obedient to God's calling in their lives? ___

And yet when we commit our children to God, and pray for Him to establish them in service to Him, we can also be confident that He will walk them through whatever they face as a result of their obedience. Check out the following and sum up each verse in your own words:

☐ 2 Corinthians 4:8-9 _____

☐ Psalm 34:19-20 _____

☐ 1 John 4:4 _____

❦   ❦   ❦

Prayer Journal

As you pray, spend a few moments in praise, confession, petition, and thanksgiving, incorporating the words of the following Scriptures into your prayers. When appropriate, personalize each verse with the pronouns "I" or "me" or with the name of your child.

❦   ❦   ❦

Regarding praise:

"I know that the Lord is great, that our Lord is greater than all gods. The Lord does whatever pleases Him, in the heavens and on the earth, in the seas and all their depths. He makes clouds rise from the ends of the earth; He sends lightning with the rain and brings out the wind from His storehouses" (Ps. 135:5-7).

❦   ❦   ❦

Regarding confession:

"Therefore confess your sins to each other and pray for each other so that you may be healed. The prayer of a righteous man is powerful and effective" (James 5:16).

❦   ❦   ❦

Regarding your request:

"I know that You can do all things; no plan of Yours can be thwarted" (Job 42:2).

Select one of the verses from the Bible study and use it as a basis for your intercession regarding your child's spiritual gifts and future ministry.

Which verse did you select? _____

How might you pray this verse for your child?

_____

_____

_____

_____

Additional topics you may want to discuss with God:

🙰 Ask God to show you some of His purposes for your child.

🙰 Ask Him to prepare you for any sacrifice that you as a parent may be asked to make as you ready your child for God's purpose in his or her life, and also as you later free him or her to fulfill that purpose.

❧ ❧ ❧

Regarding thanksgiving:

"I will praise You, O Lord, with all my heart; before the 'gods' I will sing Your praise. I will bow down toward Your holy temple and will praise Your name for Your love and Your faithfulness, for You have exalted above all things Your name and Your word. When I called, You answered me. You made me bold and stout-hearted" (Ps. 138:1-3).

❧ ❧ ❧

Space for thoughts, requests, praises, insights, a letter to God, a list of favorite verses on this topic, notes, and/or answers to prayer.

_____

_____

_____

_____

❧ ❧ ❧

SECTION 4

Praying for Your Child's Protection

DAY ~11~ Safe and Sound

" 'Because he loves Me,' says the Lord, 'I will rescue him; I will protect him, for he acknowledges My name' " (Ps. 91:4).

The physical protection of our children is of paramount importance, isn't it? After all, there are so many dangers! As a parent, many of these dangers are out of my control. Others, of course, fall well within my ability to discourage or prevent.

Or so I like to think.

Before I became a parent, I heard other moms and dads laugh, in hindsight, over tumbles their kids had survived as infants. Oh, you know the stories: this one fell off the changing table . . . that one rolled off the bed . . . another was dropped on his head by a fumbling older sibling.

I was appalled. This kind of accident was so — so — preventable! What were these parents thinking? Didn't they know *never* to leave a child alone on a bed or changing table? Didn't they know to monitor their babies in the arms of other children? I vowed to be a better parent than those around me. I would be careful. I would take charge. I would prevent unnecessary accidents. I would protect my baby.

The first time *my* infant rolled off the bed, I had stepped into the bathroom for a Kleenex. Tissue in hand, I walked back into the bedroom just in time to see Kaitlyn slide, headfirst, off the bed and hit the floor.

I screamed. Kaitlyn began to cry. I was still screaming as Larry darted into the room and summed up the crisis in one quick glance. He bent and scooped Kaitlyn into his arms just as I yelled hysterically, "Don't touch her! Her neck might be broken!"

155

About that time Kaitlyn quit crying and settled calmly into her father's arms.

Now that he had rescued Kaitlyn, it was time to calm *me* down.

So maybe I overreacted. It's just that I was so *sure* I could protect her from almost anything. I thought I had it all under control.

What a laugh!

We do our best, don't we? "No sharp instruments in the car." "Wear long pants while roller skating or riding a bike." "Don't run around the pool." "Be careful around the hot stove." "Don't talk to strangers." "Say no to drugs." "Don't use the power tools without supervision." "Don't drive and drink." "Don't drive with friends who drink." And yet tragedies can happen.

Where would we be if we couldn't commit the safety of our children into the hands of an all-knowing, all-powerful, and all-loving God? Of course, God doesn't guarantee physical safety to any of us—it is often suffering, in fact, that brings about the greatest spiritual growth. And yet we know from His Word that He can and does protect and keep us from much of the world's harm.

There is only one person who loves your child more than you do: God. As your child grows, he will increasingly move beyond the boundaries of your power to protect. Yet God's power to protect knows no boundaries. Protect your child to the best of your human abilities—then trust God with the rest.

🐛 🐛 🐛

Bible Study

As you answer the following questions, keep in mind verses you might want to "pray" over your child. When possible, copy the entire verse from your Bible verbatim or alter it slightly so it includes the name of your child.

How many hours did your child spend at school this week? (If you are in the midst of summer vacation, think back to an average schoolweek) _____

How many hours were spent at the homes of friends, neighbors, grandparents, etc.? _____

If you have small children, were they left in the care of a baby-sitter this week? If so, for how long? _____
What other events or activities separated your child from your direct supervision this week? _____

How limited is God when it comes to supervising your child? Read the following passages, selecting your favorite verse:
☐ Psalm 139:1-18 _____
_____
_____

☐ Romans 8:38 _____
_____
_____

Throughout the Bible, we read stories of men and women who were spared physical harm by divine intervention. By what means did God intervene in the following examples?
☐ Daniel 6:22 _____
☐ Acts 5:19-20 _____
☐ Matthew 2:13 _____

What do the following verses teach us about the ministry of angels?
☐ Psalm 34:7 _____
☐ Genesis 24:40 _____
☐ Psalm 91:11-12 _____
☐ Hebrews 1:7 _____
☐ Matthew 18:10 _____

God protects us through the use of ministering angels. He also protects us as we follow the precepts and principles He has set into motion. Each of the following verses contains a promise or benefit regarding physical health, safety, or length of life. It also contains a condition. Please note the benefit and condition in each verse. For example:
Psalm 34:11-14
    Benefit(s): being allowed to experience many good days

Condition(s): fear God; don't speak evil or lies; turn from evil; do good; pursue peace

Psalm 34:19
Benefit(s): deliverance from troubles and physical safety
Condition(s): we have to be righteous

Proverbs 3:1-2
Benefit(s): long life and prosperity
Condition(s): remember and follow the teachings and commands of godly parents

Your turn:
☐ Psalm 91:9-12
Benefit(s): _____
Condition(s): _____
☐ Proverbs 4:10-14
Benefit(s): _____
Condition(s): _____
☐ Exodus 20:12
Benefit(s): _____
Condition(s): _____
☐ Proverbs 16:23-24
Benefit(s): _____
Condition(s): _____

Prayer Journal

As you pray, spend a few moments in praise, confession, petition, and thanksgiving, incorporating the words of the following Scriptures into your prayers. When appropriate, personalize each verse with the pronouns "I" or "me" or with the name of your child.

Regarding praise:

"The Lord reigns, He is robed in majesty; the Lord is robed in majesty and is armed with strength. The world is firmly established; it cannot be moved. Your throne was established long ago; You are from all eternity" (Ps. 93:1-2).

Regarding confession:

"Acknowledge the God of your father, and serve Him with whole-hearted devotion and with a willing mind, for the Lord searches every heart and understands every motive behind the thoughts. If you seek Him, He will be found by you; but if you forsake Him, He will reject you forever" (1 Chron. 28:9).

Regarding our requests to God:

Select one of the verses from the Bible study. Which verse did you select? _____

How might you pray this verse for your child?

_____

_____

_____

Additional topics you may want to discuss with God:
- Ask God to surround your child with His ministering and guarding angels.
- Note the "conditions" mentioned in the Bible study—honoring parents, being righteous, pleasant words, etc.—that foster health and longevity. Ask God to develop these traits in your child.

Regarding thanksgiving:

"Come, let us bow down in worship, let us kneel before the Lord our Maker; for He is our God and we are the people of His pasture, the flock under His care" (Ps. 95:6-7).

Space for thoughts, requests, praises, insights, a letter to God, a list of favorite verses on this topic, notes, and/or answers to prayer.

_____

_____

Praying for Your Child's Protection

DAY 12 — Mind Games

"In addition to all this, take up the shield of faith, with which you can extinguish all the flaming arrows of the evil one" (Eph. 6:16).

My friend Jamie Lash plays an interesting game with his children, ages five and eight. Until he shared this story with me, I'd never heard of a game quite like it, but I've wondered since if it couldn't somehow be mass-produced and marketed.

He calls it "Fiery Darts" and no, it doesn't have anything to do with the disciplinary threats of desperate parents.

Jamie's objective is to teach his daughters to defend themselves against the battery of fiery darts that Satan directs daily at those of us who believe in Jesus Christ. It's a worthwhile objective. But what I admire most is his technique.

Picture the "tickle games" we all played with our infants and toddlers. Swooping his index finger through the air, Jamie prepares to "dive-bomb" eight-year-old Jennifer with a fiery dart. "You're not important; God doesn't love you!" he says as his finger approaches Jennifer's heart.

Jennifer, who has obviously played the game before, blocks the dart with her hand. She shouts back, "It is written: We love because He first loved us!' First John 4:19!"

Dad tries another approach. "Jennifer, you don't need to listen to your mom. What does *she* know anyway?"

Jennifer blocks the dart: "It is written: 'Children, obey your parents in the Lord, for this is right.' Ephesians 6:1."

Finally, "You're not really saved. You're not going to heaven."

Jennifer giggles as she slaps the dart away. "It is written: 'I tell you the truth, he who believes in Me has everlasting life.' John 6:47."

We can protect our children physically. But what good is physical health if their minds are consumed with the lies and myths of Satan and the world?

There are so many twisted and perverted philosophies in the world today. Satan is having a heyday with the minds of believers and nonbelievers alike as biblical values and ethics that have stood the test of time are being cast aside for the latest in philosophical fads. Imagine using politics as the standard in thought and ethics! God forbid that we should suggest a *"biblically* correct" standard of thinking for our nation. No! Far better that we should adopt *"politically* correct" standards instead!

Praying for the protection of your child *must* include praying for the protection of his mind. Sin, after all, begins with the *thought* of sinning.

A single myth or misconception—also fostered and nurtured in the mind—has the power to misguide your child for life. Satan, after all, is the father of lies. Jesus Christ, however, came to earth to connect us with truth.

Let's pray that the minds of our children would be saturated with God's truth—not twisted and crippled by Satan's lies.

🐛 🐛 🐛

Bible Study

As you answer the following questions, keep in mind verses you might want to "pray" over your child. When possible, copy the entire verse from your Bible verbatim or alter it slightly so it includes the name of your child.

What is God's will concerning the mind of your child?
☐ Romans 12:2 _____

☐ Hebrews 8:10 _____

☐ 2 Corinthians 2:16 _____

Read Ephesians 6:13-18. This passage describes the "armor" of God that we are encouraged to don, discussing, among other things, the shield of faith capable of extinguishing the flaming arrows of the enemy. How exactly do we obtain faith?

☐ Romans 10:17 _____

What else do the Scriptures have to say about the protection available to believers through the power of the Word of God?

☐ Matthew 22:29 _____
☐ Psalm 119:9, 11 _____
☐ Proverbs 30:5 _____

Other Scriptures on this subject include:

ﻌ Romans 12:2
ﻌ 2 Timothy 1:12-13
ﻌ John 8:31-32
ﻌ 1 Thessalonians 2:15
ﻌ Ephesians 4:14
ﻌ 1 Peter 5:8
ﻌ 2 Corinthians 11:3

❦ ❦ ❦

Prayer Journal

As you pray, spend a few moments in praise, confession, petition, and thanksgiving, incorporating the words of the following Scriptures into your prayers. When appropriate, personalize each verse with the pronouns "I" or "me" or with the name of your child.

Regarding praise:

"Blessed are those who have learned to acclaim You, who walk in the light of Your presence, O Lord. They rejoice in Your name all day long; they exult in Your righteousness" (Ps. 89:15-16).

❦ ❦ ❦

Regarding confession:

"You are kind and forgiving, O Lord, abounding in love to all who call to You. Hear my prayer, O Lord; listen to my cry for mercy. In the day of my trouble I will call to You, for You will answer me" (Ps. 86:5-7).

🐞 🐞 🐞

Regarding our requests to God:

Select one or more of the verses from the Bible study. Which verse did you select? _____

How might you pray this verse for your child?

_____

_____

_____

_____

Additional topics you may want to discuss with God:

🍂 That God will enable you to help your child recognize and reject the lies of the world.

🍂 That God would open *your* eyes to any lies or misconceptions you have accepted from Satan and/or from the world. The wrongful beliefs we hold together with our actions will, almost without a doubt, afflict our children as well.

🐞 🐞 🐞

Regarding thanksgiving:

"Teach me Your way, O Lord, and I will walk in Your truth; give me an undivided heart, that I may fear Your name. I will praise You, O Lord my God, with all my heart; I will glorify Your name forever" (Ps. 86:11-12).

🐞 🐞 🐞

Space for thoughts, requests, praises, insights, a letter to God, a list of favorite verses on this topic, notes, and/or answers to prayer.

_____

_____

_____

_____

🐞 🐞 🐞

Praying for Your Child's Protection

DAY 13 Sins Revealed

"You know my folly, O God; my guilt is not hidden from You" (Ps. 69:5).

Tom is a very brave man.

He's brave because he is a police officer.

He's brave because he is the father of four.

But most of all, he's brave because he dared to pray this prayer: "Lord, reveal to me any sins lurking in the lives of my children."

It's a scary prayer because God just might say, "OK." The week after praying this prayer, Tom caught one of his sons in a series of lies. Did God prompt Ryan to lie? Hardly. But He orchestrated the events that brought the lies to the attention of Ryan's father. Now that Tom knows an area in which Ryan is struggling, he is better prepared to guide, correct, and protect his son.

Let's face it: most of us don't want to know more than we have to. I mean, aren't there just some things that parents are better off not knowing about?

Larry was a highly mischievous kid. Even in college, he participated in more than his share of pranks. Unfortunately, his father was a faculty member at the Christian school he attended. Frequently during dinner, Dad Linamen would tell shocking stories of some new prank on campus, not realizing the prankster was sitting two feet away.

Only once did Larry blow his cover during one of Dad's dinner-hour sagas. Dad was explaining how some kids had climbed onto the roof of the college president's home with torches, when suddenly Larry blurted, "No, Dad, that's not what happened at all! All we had were rolls of toilet paper. Mrs. Reardon must have

164

gotten shook and called the fire station instead of the police. But there were never any torches."

Ever since I've known him, Dad Linamen has had high blood pressure.

I don't wonder how he got it.

OK, so maybe there's something to be said for not knowing *every* skeleton in our kids' closets, but still, as a rule, if we are to be successful in protecting and guiding our children, we need to be in the know.

Often, if our children are struggling with sin in their lives, they will leave clues, like breadcrumbs in the forest, telling us they need our help. Remember Vic and Bonnie? Vic remembers that — several years before their son Ronnie disappeared from home — there were signs of his involvement with drugs. His taste in music changed. His choice of friends changed. Even the decor in his room changed as posters of heavy metal bands cast dark grins and demonic glares down from the walls in Ronnie's room. Once, Bonnie discovered a cache of marijuana in Ronnie's room. Ronnie swore it belonged to his friends, and his parents let the incident pass. One year later it was too late to do anything about the signs they had seen: Ronnie was gone. He had disappeared into the underworld of drug abuse and profiteering.

Today, Vic, Bonnie, and their son have weathered the storms of Ronnie's addiction largely intact. But there are still scars. The months leading up to the reunion of their family left them racked with pain and heartache. Even the reunion itself required patience and took its toll.

Six months after Ronnie disappeared, Vic and Bonnie were driving down a wintry country road near their home when they spotted two bedraggled vagrants walking barefoot in the snow. Bonnie recognized her son almost immediately; it took Vic a moment longer.

They invited Ronnie and his girlfriend to their home for a cup of hot chocolate. To their surprise, Ronnie accepted. What happened next was perhaps the greater surprise: Vic and Bonnie spent the next two hours just loving Ronnie. There were no harsh words, no accusations or demands. They fed their son and his friend and sent them on their way with blankets and a change of clothes. The before-prayer Vic could never have shown unconditional love to his wayward son: The new and improved Vic managed to do just that. Strengthed by prayer, Vic and Bonnie swore they would never bail Ronnie out—they would let him reap the natural consequences of his choices. But they would love him unconditionally through the process.

Nearly a year passed before Ronnie asked to come home to stay. He volunteered to stay away from drugs and follow the house rules. Ronnie finished school and went on to get a job with a local contractor. Ronnie still struggles, but he is making his life work. Vic wonders, however, how things might have turned out if he had done something about the very first signs . . . the ones he saw and ignored until it was almost too late.

We don't do ourselves, or our children, any favors by ignoring the signs or by keeping ourselves ignorant of the temptations and transgressions in their lives. To make things worse, kids excel at being sneaky. In the natural, they seem to have an edge on us—there are simply too many ways to get away with too many things.

That's why we need the power of prayer to help us protect our children from the cancerous nature of hidden sins. We can ask God to sensitize us to any warning signs of dangerous behavior in our children. We can also ask him to orchestrate events that will bring into the light any dark or hidden secrets.

My parents didn't allow me to date until I was sixteen. Unfortunately, at fifteen I fell for a young man who worked for my father. My parents liked him and would have allowed us to date after my birthday—but we jumped the gun, seeing each other before and after school and even late at night. Whereas normal dating would have provided limits and supervision, "sneaking" did not.

In the midst of my deception, my praying mother knew something was wrong. She even woke me one night with her concerns. She had been praying, and her heart was burdened for me. I, of course, denied that there was anything going on in my life to be concerned about. Several months later when she came across written evidence of my relationship, it was hardly a coincidence. She had, after all, been praying for me, and I have no doubt that her discovery was prompted by God. In any case, my deceit was brought into the light and my relationship came to a sudden end. I was heartbroken. I was humbled before my parents and before God. Yet I was also relieved. Living a lie can be exhausting, even when you're fifteen.

God knows everything. Every temptation. Every slip. Every rebellious thought or destructive choice. He warns us that our sins will, one day, be brought into the light. They *will* be made known—sooner or later.

So our choices are these:

We can ignore dark secrets—in our own lives and in the lives of our children—as long as possible. We do this, of course, knowing that until the inevitable day when God will reveal the sin, it gains power and destructive force as it is nurtured in silence.

Or we can control the damage by confronting temptations and transgressions early on, before they have a chance to wreak even greater destruction.

"Lord, reveal to me any sins lurking in the lives of my children."

It seems like a scary prayer. But when you really think about it, maybe it's not. It's a lot less scary, after all, than the alternative.

❦   ❦   ❦

Bible Study

As you answer the following questions, keep in mind verses you might want to "pray" over your child. When possible, copy the entire verse from your Bible verbatim or alter it slightly so it includes the name of your child.

Is there anything going on in the life of your child of which God is not aware? What do the following verses tell us the extent of God's knowledge of us?

- ☐ 1 Samuel 16:7: God sees our _____
- ☐ 1 Chronicles 28:9: God not only searches our _____ but understands our _____
- ☐ Ezekiel 11:5: God knows _____
- ☐ Matthew 10:30: God counts our _____

Is it within our ability or the abililty of our children to hide anything—anything at all—from the eyes of our Maker? What do the following verses say to you?
☐ Isaiah 29:15-16 _____

What does God promise to do with our secret sins?
☐ 1 Samuel 2:3: God knows our _____ and will judge our _____

For the sake of your child, it is far better to have secret sins revealed and dealt with *earlier* than *later*. Other than judgment—which is bad enough!—what are some additional consequences of hidden sin?
☐ According to Jeremiah 5:25, what is withheld from the man, woman, or child with hidden sin in his or her life? _____

☐ According to Isaiah 59:2, sin also causes _____
☐ Another consequence of long-term hidden sin in the life of your child may be actual physical distress. We all know, after all, the physical results that can be harvested from emotional—and even spiritual—stress. What do the following verses say about this?
☐ Psalm 38:3 _____
☐ Lamentations 1:20 _____

Is anyone without sin? First John 1:8 says that if we say we have no sin in our lives, we are liars. Yet what is available to us and to our children despite—and even because of—the sin in our lives?
☐ 1 John 1:9 _____
☐ Isaiah 1:18 _____
☐ Psalm 103:12 _____

In Job 13:23 Job prays: "How many wrongs and sins have I committed? Show me my offense and my sin." I believe we can pray this prayer for our children, asking God to bring their offenses into the light. Let's ask God to bring these things to the attention of our children so that they can repent, or to our attention so we can encourage repentance. By doing this, we help protect our children from the damaging fruits and ramifications of hidden sin in their lives.

❦   ❦   ❦

Prayer Journal

As you pray, spend a few moments in praise, confession, petition, and thanksgiving, incorporating the words of the following Scriptures into your prayers. When appropriate, personalize each verse with the pronouns "I" or "me" or with the name of your child.

Regarding praise:

"Shout for joy, O heavens; rejoice, O earth; burst into song, O mountains! For the Lord comforts His people and will have compassion on His afflicted ones" (Isa. 49:13).

❦   ❦   ❦

Regarding confession:

"Seek the Lord while He may be found; call on Him while He is near. Let the wicked forsake his way and the evil man his thoughts. Let him turn to the Lord, and He will have mercy on him, and to our God, for He will freely pardon" (Isa. 55:6-7).

❦   ❦   ❦

Regarding your request:

Select one of the verses from the Bible study and use it as a basis for your intercession regarding any hidden sins or temptations in the life of your child. Which verse did you select? _____
How might you pray this verse for your child?

_____
_____
_____

Additional topics you may want to discuss with God:
❧ As believers, we are never free from the enticements of sin. Learning to recognize sin in our lives, repenting of our sins, resubmitting our hearts and souls to the lordship of Jesus

Christ, and accepting His forgiveness in our lives are processes we will need to embrace our entire lives. Sin in your life—and in the life of your child—is not catastrophic. It is, on the contrary, unavoidable. One of our goals as parents is not to demand our children to be sinless, but to teach them how to respond to those inevitable moments when they will look into their own souls and wince at what they find. Ask God to help you and your child focus on the importance of learning the *process* of dealing with sin.

❦   ❦   ❦

Regarding thanksgiving:

"Let them give thanks to the Lord for His unfailing love and His wonderful deeds for men, for He satisfies the thirsty and fills the hungry with good things" (Ps. 107:8-9).

❦   ❦   ❦

Space for thoughts, requests, praises, insights, a letter to God, a list of favorite verses on this topic, notes, and/or answers to prayer.

_____

_____

_____

_____

_____

_____

_____

_____

_____

_____

_____

_____

_____

_____

_____

_____

❦   ❦   ❦

SECTION 5

Characteristics God Wants to Develop in Your Child

DAY 14 — Taming of the Tongue

"He who guards his mouth and his tongue keeps himself from calamity" (Prov. 21:23).

A man once told me that he had virtually stopped going to the movie theater. He also had begun to exercise great care when renting movie videos. His new self-control had started when he noticed something rather disconcerting about himself: after years of watching his favorite movie-diet of thrillers, westerns, and other action-packed fare, this godly man and strong believer had begun to . . . well . . . pick up the language.

It's an easy thing to do in a society where four-letter-words, sexual innuendos, and other course language have been welcomed into the mainstream like never before.

Then there's the current phenomena of verbal-vomit television and tell-all journalism. You know what I'm talking about: shows and stories that are meant to shock and titillate by their no-holds-barred verbal barrage. It's nearly impossible to flip through the television channels, for example, without happening on one show or another where everyday people are addressing the nation with miniscule details about their divorces, affairs, family feuds, or sexual preferences.

Finally, haven't you noticed that it's open season on Christians and on traditional and/or biblical values? Without making a conscious effort to do otherwise, it's easy to pick up on the concepts and phrases being propagated by our godless society. Whether we're telling an off-color joke, repeating a hot piece of gossip, slipping into a lie to save our skins at work or home, or buying into the rhetoric about all that we deserve to have/be/feel, it's far too easy to start sounding just like the crowd.

And don't even get me started on kids who are disrespectful to their parents. It's a national epidemic. I mean, we never talked that way to *our* parents . . . did we?

Face it. We're raising our children in a culture where godly communication is an endangered species. On radio, television, in print, during and after school, our children are exposed to great quantities of words and messages that are anything but godly!

And yet godly communication is one of the traits that our Heavenly Father wants to develop in each of our children. It might seem easier, after a long day at the office or an exhausting day home with the kids, to simply wince and overlook inappropriate language, tones, or messages coming from the mouths of our precious babes. Yet I believe it is God's will for us, through our actions and our prayers, to grasp hold of the responsibility of instilling within our children a desire to please God with their words.

This is one of the areas we are working on with Kaitlyn. To help her develop godly communication we have instituted "The Marble Jar." There are actually two jars: one is filled with marbles, and the other is designed for Kaitlyn to fill with marbles. Each time she handles a disappointment with a respectful tone instead of a whine, she gets to move a marble from the first jar into the second. Each time she remembers the polite way to ask for something she wants, she gets to move another marble. If she follows a series of instructions—like getting dressed in the morning, or preparing for bed at night—she gets to transfer three to five marbles, depending on the tasks. When I find her and her playmates negotiating cooperative resolutions to squabbles, they each get to transfer a marble.

On the other hand, when my daughter is disrespectful, whiny, rebellious, or rude, she must remove a marble from the second jar. Some days she makes progress and the second jar gains more marbles than it loses; other days she loses ground. When the jar is filled, of course, there is a reward.

Of course, this does lead to some humorous moments. Yesterday, for example, we were in a department store when Kaitlyn resorted to some snappy back talk. "That's it," I said crisply.

"You've lost a marble." A balding man in line behind me flashed a puzzled look across his face, and I couldn't help but read his mind: *Is that supposed to be some sort of punishment? Maybe the kid's not the one with the missing marbles. . . .*

Nevertheless, this is one of the ways God is answering *my* prayers to hear godly communication from the mouths of my children: He is, in a sense, allowing me to play a part in bringing about the answer to my prayer.

How might God use you to develop this trait in your child? Like me, you may want to begin by asking God for wisdom. Then ask Him to give you a plan that will encourage your child to learn the art of godly communication. Finally, you may want to make a third request as you ask Him to help you with any ungodly communication posing a struggle in *your* life.

Now maybe you could answer a question for me:

Do snotty remarks to bald strangers count?

🍎 🍎 🍎

Bible Study

As you answer the following questions, keep in mind verses you might want to "pray" over your child. When possible, copy the entire verse from your Bible verbatim or alter it slightly so it includes the name of your child.

Why is the bridling of the tongue so important to God? One of the reasons is that the tongue is irrevocably intertwined with the heart. What do the following verses tell us about the relationship between the tongue and the heart?

☐ Proverbs 16:23 _____

_____

☐ Luke 6:45 _____

☐ Matthew 12:34-35 _____

_____

Scripture makes it clear that the words of our mouths make known the true nature of our hearts. Yet the tongue not only reflects what is in the heart, the tongue can influence the heart, soul, and body as well. What do the following verses tell us about this:

☐ Proverbs 18:20 tells us that our words are like _____

_____

☐ James 3:2 tells us that by controlling our words we can control _____

☐ James 3:5-6 tells us that the tongue has the power to defile not just the heart but _____

What are some of the benefits or promises attached to godly communication? What about the ramifications of ungodly communication? Many of the following verses list both benefit and ramification; others identify one or the other. Several of the verses have been capsulated for you—summarize what you learn from the others:

Scripture:	Godly speech:	Ungodly speech:
Proverbs 13:2	brings good things	brings a craving for violence
Proverbs 12:18	brings healing	pierces like a sword
Proverbs 13:3		
Proverbs 17:9		
Proverbs 18:6-7	— — —	brings strife & invites violence & danger
Ecclesiastes 9:17	is to be heeded	is to be ignored
Matthew 12:36-37		

What kind of communication is pleasing to God? The following verses describe God's will for our tongues. In the interest of time, the first several have been completed; the last is up to you:

☐ Proverbs 6:16-17, 19. God despises, among other things: *a lying tongue* and someone who *pours out lies and/or stirs up dissension among brothers.*

☐ Proverbs 15:1. We are to *turn away wrath with gentle answers* and to avoid *harsh words that stir up anger.*

☐ Proverbs 17:9 and 18:8 warn us to avoid *gossiping and telling confidences.*

☐ Romans 1:29-30: Which of these forms of unrighteousness have to do with the tongue? _____

Prayer Journal

As you pray, spend a few moments in praise, confession, petition, and thanksgiving, incorporating the words of the following Scriptures into your prayers. When appropriate, personalize each verse with the pronouns "I" or "me" or with the name of your child.

Regarding praise:

"Shout with joy to God, all the earth! Sing to the glory of His name; offer Him glory and praise. Say to God, 'How awesome are Your deeds! So great is Your power that Your enemies cringe before You. All the earth bows down to You; they sing praise to You, they sing praise to Your name' " (Ps. 66:1-4).

Regarding confession:

"Seek the Lord while He may be found; call on Him while He is near. Let the wicked forsake his way and the evil man his thoughts. Let him turn to the Lord, and He will have mercy on him, and to our God, for He will freely pardon" (Isa. 55:6-7).

Regarding our requests to God:

"Let your conversation be always full of grace, seasoned with salt, so that you may know how to answer everyone" (Col. 4:6).

"Set a guard before my mouth, O Lord; keep watch over the door of my lips" (Ps. 141:3).

Select one or both of the above verses to paraphrase in your prayers, inserting the name of your son or daughter as you ask God to accomplish these things in the life of your child. How might you pray this verse or verses for your child?

_____
_____
_____

Additional topics you may want to discuss with God:

🍃 Specify the kind of godly communication you want God to develop in your child, identifying any communication patterns that need to be brought into submission: Is your child disrespectful? Is he or she prone to curse or use foul language? Does he or she have a problem with lying? Is your child critical of others? Does she gossip?

🍃 Ask God for wisdom in helping your child learn godly communication. God may, after all, desire to use you as the change-agent in your child's life.

🍃 As you ask God to develop godly communication in your child, pray these same verses for your own life. Children learn by what they see and hear—if your communication with your child or others is critical, harsh, or disrepectful, you are sabotaging your own prayers! Practice what you pray! Your child will never bring his or her tongue under submission to the Holy Spirit if *your* tongue is renegade.

Regarding thanksgiving:

"Let the peace of Christ rule in your hearts, since as members of one body you were called to peace. And be thankful. Let the word of Christ dwell in you richly as you teach and admonish one another with all wisdom, and as you sing psalms, hymns and spiritual songs with gratitude in your hearts to God" (Col. 3:15-16).

Space for thoughts, requests, praises, insights, a letter to God, a list of favorite verses on this topic, notes and/or answers to prayer.

_____
_____

Characteristics God Wants to Develop in Your Child

DAY 15 — Newness of Spirit and Mind

"Therefore, if anyone is in Christ, he is a new creation; the old has gone, the new has come!" (2 Cor. 5:17)

Recently my parents and my sister Michelle flew to Texas for a visit. The two women flew commercially—my dad, however, was more adventuresome and made the trek in his small aircraft, a Piper Archer II. Kaitlyn, of course, was ecstatic to see her aunt and grandparents and excited about the new adventures the week held. One of the highlights for her was taking her first flight in a small plane with her dad and granddad.

The other highlight was going to tea.

It was Michelle's idea. So one afternoon we four "girls" got all dressed-up and drove to the Crescent Hotel in downtown Dallas. The hotel contains an antique shop, the second floor of which is a colorful tearoom brimming with porcelain dolls, teddy bears, Tiffany lamps, framed prints of English gardens and dusty volumes of Charles Dickens.

Drinking berry tea from whimical rosebud teacups, we caught up on the details of each others' lives. Even Kaitlyn, dressed in a floral dress and white gloves, had a story to share. She'd learned it in children's church and recited it with great enthusiasm. It was all about the pastor of our church's children's ministry, and how he used to own a beat-up car, and every day on his way to work drove past a car lot and coveted the new cars. Kaitlyn said it just like that—coveted—and my mother, sister, and I smiled broadly at how grown-up she sounded as she repeated the story verbatim.

After filling up on scones, cucumber sandwiches, and dainty chocolates, we left our table to browse the treasures of the tearoom. One corner, in particular, held Kaitlyn's attention. It was, of course, the nook filled with dolls and bears and picture books. Child-sized Queen Anne furniture beckoned from around the room. Dainty tea sets invited company. Beatrix Potter books and prints dotted the tables and walls.

Kaitlyn was enthralled. I was in the process of deflecting a barrage of questions beginning with the words, "Mama, can I *please* have . . ." when suddenly Kaitlyn stopped. Her hand still in mine, she looked up at me, an expression of surprise on her face.

"Mama," she whispered, "I think I'm coveting this room."

A small insight. A spiritual truth. It began as a funny story heard in children's church, and yet that seemingly innocuous tale contained the seed of revelation for my six-year-old. Seeing her standing there, jam on her collar and surprise in her eyes, I wanted to laugh. And I wanted to cry.

The Bible tells us that we are new creatures in Christ. It is a wonderful gift, this renewal of our very minds and spirits, and I am acquainted with it well: I understand that the Holy Spirit works quietly to harvest change in our hearts and souls, and I know full well what God has managed to accomplish in my own often stubborn life.

But nothing prepares you for the rush of joy and gratitude that comes from seeing the Holy Spirit at work in the life of your child.

I used to think how wonderful it would be to have perfect children. Now I know how much they would miss by being too good. I don't want perfect children: I want something far better for them than that! I want them to know the power of the Holy Spirit, to feel God's hand of change in their lives, and to recognize the depth of their need for the blood of Jesus Christ.

I want them to know the power of renewal.

❦   ❦   ❦

Bible Study

As you answer the following questions, keep in mind verses you might want to "pray" over your child. When possible, copy the entire verse from your Bible verbatim or alter it slightly so it includes the name of your child.

Renewal. Regeneration. Sanctification. Whatever we call it, submitting to the life-changing work of the Holy Spirit in our hearts and minds is not an overnight process. What does the following verse tell us about God's patience and dedication in completing the work He has begun in each of us? Until what day will He continue our renewal and sanctification?

☐ Philippians 1:6: _____

Why does God bring about the renewal and regeneration of our sinful hearts and minds?

☐ Romans 12:2: Because it is the _____
☐ Ezekiel 11:19-20: So that what four things might occur:
    1. _____
    2. _____
    3. _____
    4. _____
☐ Acts 26:18: So that we might receive _____
and _____
☐ Jeremiah 31:3: Ultimately, God draws us and sanctifies us because He _____

How does God bring about the renewal and regeneration of our sinful hearts and minds?

☐ Ezekiel 11:19: God gives us what three things: *an undivided heart, new spirit and a heart of flesh,* and He takes away *our hearts of stone.*
☐ Ezekiel 36:27: He places within us His own *Spirit.*
☐ 1 Corinthians 6:11: We are washed, sanctified, and justified through what two relationships: _____ and
_____
☐ 2 Corinthians 5:17: We are new creatures when we are _
_____
☐ 2 Peter 1:3: We are brought into godliness through *His divine power,* and we are called to glory and virtue through our *His own glory and goodness.*
☐ 1 John 5:4-5: We can overcome the world when we are _

and when we believe _____

And how do we become born of God? See 1 John 5:1: _____

_____

Knowing these things, what might your prayer be for your child? With whom must your child have a relationship before God can begin to bring renewal in his or her life? _____

It is God's will for your child to accept the saving work of Jesus Christ and to know God through Jesus Christ. (See Matt. 18:14.) Is your child a believer? _____

If you have any question about whether your child has opened the lid of his heart, so to speak, and welcomed in Jesus Christ as Lord, then make this a matter of prayer. Talk to your child. Pray with your child.

Do you remember Gerald Garcia, the Young Life director mentioned in chapter 1? I really appreciated his perspective: he was, of course, concerned about the behavior of all of the teens he came in contact with—yet when he met a kid who didn't know the Lord, Gerald's first priority was not to chastise a teen for smoking, for example, but to introduce him or her to Jesus Christ. Gerald's immediate goal was not to change behavior, but the heart.

When my dad was a young man, just home from the service, he had pulled away from the teachings of his Christian parents and was not living for the Lord. One night after dinner he pulled on his jacket, grabbed his car keys and, whistling, was headed out the front door when an friend of the family hollered from the kitchen table where he still sat with my grandparents: "Have a good time, son!"

My dad stopped at the front door and turned around, shaking his head good-naturedly as he spoke. "Uncle Will, you know I'm going out drinking with my buddies. And yet you're telling me to have a good time!"

Uncle Will nodded. "That's right, son. While you serve the devil, serve him with all you got. But when you become a Christian, serve God with all you've got too."

We have a lot of expectations for our children. Yet without a saving relationship with Jesus Christ, they—like you and me—are sinful, selfish beings. Their salvation must precede their sanctification—their behavior cannot be "renewed" when their hearts are not.

We have some control, of course, over the behavior of our small children. I am not suggesting that parents stop insisting on manners or appropriate behavior—this is, indeed, how we teach our children.

But when our small children turn into young adults and begin making decisions of their own, it will not be *our* desires (or threats of discipline) that guide their actions, but the nature and desires of their own hearts. Encourage godly behavior—but pay special attention to the health of the heart of your child.

As our children move beyond salvation and begin to experience sanctification, what evidences will begin to appear in their lives? How will their behavior show the change in their hearts? Drawing from the following passages, are there any behaviors your child is struggling with at this time? If so, commit to pray about these. Also pray about the behaviors you want to see God develop in your child, knowing that it is God's will for your child to exercise these traits. How might you personalize the following passages and incorporate them into your prayers for your child?

☐ Galatians 5:19-25 _____

_____

_____

_____

_____

_____

_____

_____

☐ Colossians 3:12-17 _____

_____

_____

_____

_____
_____
_____
_____

❦ ❦ ❦

Prayer Journal

As you pray, spend a few moments in praise, confession, petition, and thanksgiving, incorporating the words of the following Scriptures into your prayers. When appropriate, personalize each verse with the pronouns "I" or "me" or with the name of your child.

Regarding praise:

"O Lord, You are my God; I will exalt You and praise Your name, for in perfect faithfulness You have done marvelous things, things planned long ago" (Isa. 25:1).

❦ ❦ ❦

Regarding confession:

"He who conceals his sins does not prosper, but whoever confesses and renounces them finds mercy" (Prov. 28:13).

❦ ❦ ❦

Regarding our requests to God:

Select one or more of the verses found in Galatians 5:19-25 and/or Colossians 3:12-14. Personalize the verse(s) to represent your prayer on behalf of your child. Now or in the near future, you may want to select a single area in which your child needs to develop the mind of Christ, then locate and pray Scriptures that relate specifically to that area.

Which verse did you select? _____

How might you pray this verse for your child?

_____
_____
_____
_____

❦ ❦ ❦

Regarding thanksgiving:

"But thanks be to God! He gives us the victory though our Lord Jesus Christ" (1 Cor. 15:57).

❦   ❦   ❦

Space for thoughts, requests, praises, insights, a letter to God, a list of favorite verses on this topic, notes, and/or answers to prayer.

_____

_____

_____

_____

_____

_____

_____

_____

_____

_____

_____

_____

_____

_____

_____

_____

_____

_____

_____

_____

_____

_____

_____

_____

_____

_____

_____

_____

_____

_____

❦   ❦   ❦

Characteristics God Wants to Develop in Your Child

DAY 16 — Sexual Purity

"Flee from sexual immorality" (1 Cor. 6:18).

No one can deny that we live in a society saturated with sexual images and messages. From billboards and movies, music and television, friends and even the other adults in their lives, our children are bombarded daily with information and values regarding sex. As parents, the task of helping our children develop godly values and healthy attitudes about sexuality is a profound privilege. It can also be a significant challenge!

    Kindergartners in a school in New York are learning about homosexual "families" through books with titles such as *Heather Has Two Mommies* in which a girl lives with her mother and her mother's lesbian lover.

    A sixth-grade girl I know complained after a health teacher demonstrated how to use a condom using a cucumber.

    We met with friends this weekend whose sixteen-year-old daughter quit attending a *church youth group* where she was being taught that, as long as she is careful, sexual experimentation is a normal part of growing up.

    Finally, have you watched network or cable television lately?

As praying, Christian parents, we can't be afraid to talk to our children about sex and sexual values. After all, no one else in their lives seems to hestitate!

When I think of praying for Kaitlyn in this area, I think first of praying for wisdom for myself. There are three goals that I believe parents can set for themselves as they seek to—as Tipper Gore described in the title of a book she authored—*Raising PG Kids in an X-Rated Society.*

184

Our first goal is to protect our children, as much as possible, from being misinformed or over-informed about sexual issues. Last week my friend Cherie Spurlock was petitioned by her fifteen-year-old son, Daniel, who wanted to see a movie with his friends. Cherie, who had already seen the movie in question, knew that the opening scenes included a provocative bedroom encounter. She gave Daniel permission to see the movie—on one condition. He had to leave the theater just before and during the rather heated scene.

Daniel handled the stipulation with finesse: after he and his buddies found their seats, Daniel collected money and orders from his friends and hit the snack bar. By the time he returned ladened with popcorn and Pepsi, the steam had cleared from the screen and all the breathing in the theater had returned to normal.

I was impressed with how Daniel handled the situation. I was also impressed with Cherie for setting the condition in the first place. It's not always easy to make—and enforce—such a stand in today's sex-saturated society.

Second, even as we monitor the sexual messages and images our children might be exposed to from the outside world, we need to make sure that we are accessible sources of godly values and healthy information about sexuality and the act of sex.

I believe in answering all of my children's questions about sex at the moment the question is posed. I will never say, "When you're older. . . ." If they are asking, they have a need to know, and if I don't answer, they'll find someone who will.

I also believe in including whatever details they ask for. Of course, any details they *don't* ask about are at my discretion to disclose or to save until later.

This philosophy has served me well . . . until last week. This was the week when Kaitlyn's curiosity led her beyond the boundaries of our previous discussions. Suddenly it wasn't enough to know that babies were created when daddies put seeds inside of the mommies. Suddenly my six-year-old wanted to know where the dads got these seeds, and exactly how they transferred them inside their wives!

My husband walked into the room as Kaitlyn and I were winding down our discussion. Kaitlyn promptly announced, "I know

185

that you and Mama have *sex!*" She went on to ask for a brother or sister, and suggested that Larry and I have sex the next day when she was in school.

OK, I admit it. Open communication on these issues can feel uncomfortable at the time. It can also lead into some humorously embarrassing moments. But if we don't talk to our children about sex, about AIDS, about masturbation, about dating temptations, who will? Do we really trust Oprah or the bedroom-eyed teens on "Beverly Hills 90210" to teach our children what we want them to know about sex?

We need to be accessible. We also need to make sure the messages we send are healthy:

ða When we scold a toddler for discovering parts of his body that are, admittedly, pretty interesting, what message are we sending?

ða When our kids ask us about sex and we turn beet-red and change the subject, what have we taught them?

ða If we always talk about the negatives of premarital sex — and forget to mention the joy and miracle of sex within the haven of marriage — how long will we have our children's ears? How credible will they view us? After all, their own bodies are telling them sex is something good and enjoyable. Why should they listen to the no-fun pictures we paint?

ða If we women enjoy verbally bashing the insensitive men in our lives — or men resort to sexist jokes or comments — what impact have we had on the gender identity of our children? How have we encouraged negative gender stereotypes in their minds?

Finally, we need to prepare our children for the time when we can no longer shield them from the wealth of misinformation about human sexuality that our world has to offer. After all, we can't protect them forever. We have to, somehow, help them internalize healthy perspectives and biblical values, so they can make wise choices on their own. Inititially we need to shield them from misinformation — eventually we need to help them recognize and avoid it.

As we pray for our children to develop godly values and identities as sexual beings, let's also keep in mind that part of God's design is for our children to learn these values by *our* words and examples. The best results will come when we couple our prayers with our own efforts. We need to *pray*—but we also need to *act,* protecting our children from misinformation, being accessible and generous with godly information, and preparing them to discern wisely between the two.

ಀ ಀ ಀ

Bible Study

As you answer the following questions, keep in mind verses you might want to "pray" over your child. When possible, copy the entire verse from your Bible verbatim or alter it slightly so it includes the name of your child.

As we encourage our children to remain sexually pure until marriage, what reasons do we give them? If we use only the reasoning of the world—"Unprotected sex can lead to AIDS or pregnancy"—then they will be suspectible to the world's solutions—"Condoms and abortions are your tickets to safe sex!"

There's nothing wrong with talking about the societal ills that come from illicit sexual activity. But don't stop there. What standards does God give us, and what are His reasons for these standards? Read 1 Corinthians 6:18-20 and answer the following questions:

ೆ What does God want us to do when faced with sexual temptation?

_____

ೆ Why is sexual immorality so dangerous? _____

_____

ೆ Why are we to protect our bodies from sexual immorality?

_____

What higher calling does God have for us? _____

_____

Do your children understand the stepping-stones from temptation to immorality? These verses may help you explain the sequence to your children:

ೆ The question is not what to do if we are tempted, but *when* we are tempted. We all face temptation. Neither is it a sin to be tempted. Fleeting lusts, rebellious thoughts, or desires are some-

187

thing we experience throughout our lives.
- ☐ 1 Corinthians 10:13 _____

࿇ We can't control what lustful thoughts or temptations come knocking at our door—but we can decide whether or not to invite them in for dinner! Dwelling on rebellious desires, acting out these desires in our minds, or replaying past sins are all dangerous activities! Why? Based on the following verse, how powerful are our thoughts? (Keep in mind that the word "look" in this verse is often translated "gaze" or even "gaze with longing.")
- ☐ Matthew 5:28 _____

࿇ What are the consequences of the sinful actions borne from our rebellious thoughts?
- ☐ James 1:13-15 _____

How can we resist sexual temptation?
- ☐ How did Joseph resist temptation in Genesis 39:6-12?

- ☐ What does Proverbs 4:14-15 teach us about the art of removing ourselves physically from the presence of temptation:

- ☐ What three key words enabled Jesus to resist temptation in Matthew 4:1-11 as He used the knowledge of Scripture to ward off Satan's attack? _____
- ☐ What does Ephesians 6:11-17 tell us about the strategy for resisting temptation? Note in particular verse 14. How are we to protect, figuratively speaking, the heart of our sexuality? What are we to buckle around our waist? _____

Sexual immorality is, perhaps more than any other sin, grounded in deceit. Surrounding and girding ourselves with truth instead of deceit is one way to resist sexual temptation, and the Word of God is a significant source of truth.
- ☐ In Matthew 26:38-39, the natural man in Jesus would have liked to avoid the ordeal of crucifixion. What did He do in order

to bring His will into line with the will of His Father? _____
In 26:41, Christ encourages Peter to use this same resource in his
own battles against temptation. What does He say? _____

☐ What do the following verses teach us about the value of
fellowship and accountability as a means of resisting temptation?
    ☐ 1 Thessalonians 5:14 _____

Physically removing yourself from the path of temptation, drawing strength from the Word of God, prayer, and accountability.
These are invaluable weapons against temptation, sexual or otherwise. Use them in your own life; teach them to your children.

Finally, make sure your child understands that God has placed
sex safely within marriage, not to punish or deny us, but to protect us and to ensure that our sexual expression brings us the
greatest pleasure possible. How has God provided for our sensual
pleasure?
    ☐ Proverbs 5:18-19 _____

    ☐ Genesis 2:18-25 _____

    ☐ Hebrews 13:4 _____

Finally, I encourage you to read the Song of Songs, today if you
have the time, or in the near future as you continue to pray for
your child to experience his or her sexuality in ways intended by
God. Many people view God as being "anti-sex"—and yet this
couldn't be further from the truth! Our sexuality is something to
be celebrated, and your child needs to be aware of God's provi-
sions for the vibrant expression of his or her sexuality.

❧ ❧ ❧

Prayer Journal
*As you pray, spend a few moments in praise, confession, petition, and
thanksgiving, incorporating the words of the following Scriptures into*

your prayers. When appropriate, personalize each verse with the pronouns "I" or "me" or with the name of your child.

Regarding praise:

"Amen! Praise and glory and wisdom and thanks and honor and power and strength be to our God forever and ever. Amen" (Rev. 7:12).

Regarding confession:

"Have mercy on me, O God, according to Your unfailing love; according to Your great compassion blot out my transgressions. Wash away all my iniquity and cleanse me from my sin. For I know my transgressions, and my sin is always before me. Against You, You only, have I sinned and done what is evil in Your sight, so that You are proved right when You speak and justified when You judge. . . . Cleanse me with hyssop, and I will be clean; wash me, and I will be whiter than snow. Let me hear joy and gladness; let the bones You have crushed rejoice. Hide Your face from my sins and blot out all my iniquity" (Ps. 51:1-4, 7-9).

Regarding our requests to God:

Select one of the verses from the Bible study and use it as a basis for your intercession regarding your relationship with your child.

Which verse did you select? _____

How might you pray this verse for your child?

_____

_____

_____

Additional topics you may want to discuss with God:

☙ Ask for wisdom as you help your child chart safe and godly paths in a dangerous and perverted world.

☙ Ask God to bring about opportunities for you and your child to talk about sex. Ask God to alert you to any dangerous philosophies your child may be buying into, or any current temptations she may need your help in overcoming.

🍎 Pray that God would protect your child from friends and peers who might encourage or pressure your child into sexual experimentation.

🍎 If you suspect or discover that your child has already yielded to sexual temptation, ask God for strength and wisdom before reacting. Ask God to bring your child to repentance and to give you wisdom to know how to talk to your child about God's forgiveness and strength for future choices.

Regarding thanksgiving:
"I am like an olive tree flourishing in the house of God; I trust in God's unfailing love forever and ever. I will praise You forever for what You have done; in Your name I will hope, for Your name is good. I will praise You in the presence of your saints" (Ps. 52:8-9).

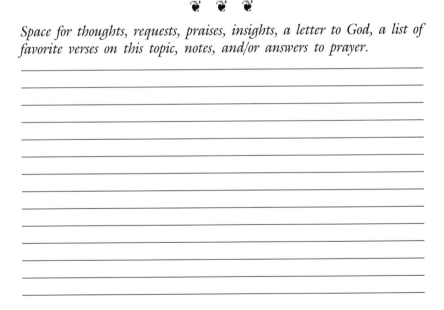

Space for thoughts, requests, praises, insights, a letter to God, a list of favorite verses on this topic, notes, and/or answers to prayer.

Characteristics God Wants to Develop in Your Child

 **DAY 17** **Patience**

"Be patient with everyone" (1 Thessalonians 5:14).

Kaitlyn and I were sitting on the couch, just having finished reading a small stack of books. I decided this Kodak moment was the perfect time to bring up a small matter I wanted to discuss.

"Kaitlyn, I wanted to thank you for all your cooperation last week when Momie and Poppy and Aunt Shelly were visiting." (Momie and Poppy are names for grandparents. Don't ask. It's a long story.)

"You're welcome."

"You were helpful and you had a good attitude. But there is something I think we need to work on."

Kaitlyn looked at me blankly. I continued: "You get frustrated too quickly when things don't go your way. Like when you're playing with your friends, or when I ask you to do something you don't want to do, and we need to work on that."

Suddenly she burst into animation. "But Mom, it's because I get impatient!"

"I know. But that doesn't make it OK behavior. You have to *learn* to be patient. If you don't, it'll cause you problems all your life."

"You don't understand," she explained. "It's like I have twenty patiences. And when they're gone, they're gone!" Her hands flew up in a shrug.

"Twenty, huh?" I smiled. Where do kids get this stuff? "Well, I'm going to help you. Together, we're going to pray that God gives you . . . oh . . . let's say, forty. Forty patiences. What d'ya say?"

Her eyes got big. "Forty? Wow!"

She's too young to know that one of the things you never pray for is patience. Of course, we all value patience—but no one wants to go through the training it takes to get any.

But this, after all, is the advantage of age and experience: I know this and she doesn't. So now we're praying for Kaitlyn to grow in patience. I'll let you know how it turns out—if there are any survivors left to tell the story.

A German proverb says it well: Patience is a bitter plant, but it bears sweet fruit. No one enjoys the trials that produce patience—and yet think how hard life would be if we spent all our days impatiently frustrated! It seems we're always waiting for one thing or another. Life is filled with delays and postponements. Unless we learn to live with patience for the things we don't have, and contentment with the things we do, we will never really live at all.

How many patiences does your child have? As a model and example for your child, how many patiences do *you* have? And maybe a better question is this: How brave are you? Praying that God would develop patience in you and/or your child is seen by some as an open door to trials and frustrations! And who knows? There may be some truth there. Yet of one thing we can be certain: your prayer also summons the help of the Holy Spirit who will help you as you pursue this godly characteristic in your life and in the life of your child.

❦ ❦ ❦

Bible Study

As you answer the following questions, keep in mind verses you might want to "pray" over your child. When possible, copy the entire verse from your Bible verbatim or alter it slightly so it includes the name of your child.

What does God use to develop patience in our lives?
☐ James 1:3 _____
☐ Romans 5:3 _____

God uses the circumstances around us to develop patience, yet patience is also the result of our choices. We can choose to be patient, or we can choose to be rash. What is the verb in the following verse that defines what our attitude should be toward patience?
☐ 1 Timothy 6:11 _____

What are the benefits that come when we excercise our patience?
☐ Romans 5:3-4 _____
☐ Hebrews 10:36 _____
☐ James 1:4 _____

Second Peter 1:5-7 gives a "Home Depot Do-It-Yourself" perspective on Christianity. With faith as the foundation, what seven elements—patience included—are we instructed to add to our faith? _____
_____

According to 2 Peter 1:8, what advantage is ours when we, indeed, begin to experience these seven traits in our lives? _____
_____

What does 2 Peter 1:9 say about about the man, woman, or child who neglects to nuture these seven traits in his or her life?
_____

If this sounds like a tough assignment, don't despair! Read 2 Peter 1:3-4 and you'll discover that God has given us all that we need to succeed in building a strong, working faith. This passage should give us every confidence that we have been, indeed, equipped for all that God requires of us. Summarize this passage in your own words: _____
_____

🍎 🍎 🍎

Prayer Journal

As you pray, spend a few moments in praise, confession, petition, and thanksgiving, incorporating the words of the following Scriptures into your prayers. When appropriate, personalize each verse with the pronouns "I" or "me" or with the name of your child.

Regarding praise:

"In God we make our boast all day long, and we will praise Your name forever" *(Ps. 44:8)*.

Regarding confession:

"Do not withhold Your mercy from me, O Lord; may Your love and Your truth always protect me. For troubles without number surround me; my sins have overtaken me, and I cannot see. They are more than the hairs of my head, and my heart fails within me. Be pleased, O Lord, to save me; O Lord, come quickly to help me" (Ps. 40:11-13).

Regarding our requests to God:

Select one of the verses from the Bible study, and use it as a basis for your intercession regarding the development of patience in your child and even in you as a parent. Which verse did you select? _____

How might you pray this verse for your child?

_____
_____
_____

Additional topics you may want to discuss with God:

🍂 You are your child's best textbook. Pray that God will develop patience in your child, but also ask Him to enhance your effectiveness as an example for your child.

🍂 Ask God to make you more aware of opportunities to point out to your child the good things that come to those who know how to wait.

🍂 Ask God to help you be a sympathetic ear if your child needs to talk about the disappointments or hardships of waiting. Without encouraging whining—heaven forbid! There's enough of that at my house already! We can help our children find appropriate ways to express their feelings. Learning patience is hard—sugarcoating this fact won't make it go away. Even David had times when he wrote about the hardships of being patient or enduring trials—yet he always managed to praise God even in the midst of expressing his emotions!

🍎 🍎 🍎

Regarding thanksgiving:
"Praise be to the Lord, to God our Savior, who daily bears our burdens" (Ps. 68:19).

🍎 🍎 🍎

Space for thoughts, requests, praises, insights, a letter to God, a list of favorite verses on this topic, notes, and/or answers to prayer.

_____

_____

_____

_____

_____

_____

_____

_____

_____

_____

_____

_____

_____

_____

_____

_____

_____

_____

_____

🍎 🍎 🍎

Characteristics God Wants to Develop in Your Child

DAY 18

Fear of the Lord

"The fear of the Lord is the beginning of knowledge"
(Prov. 1:7).

We have cable television, and this afternoon I watched the Nickelodeon channel. You know the one—"The First Network for Kids!" Nickelodeon hosts a lot of great shows that Kaitlyn is allowed to watch. But their show entitled "You Can't Do That on Television" doesn't happen to be one of them.

I am not a prude. But there is something awry with a program on which a mother feeds her children leeches for dinner, and a short-order cook makes vomit-burgers to order. I've never, in fact, seen an adult on this program represented as even remotely intelligent or reasonable or compassionate.

I know, I know. That's the whole point of the show. Maybe kids need to feel like, in a world populated by grown-ups, they can come out on top once in a while. And maybe when Kaitlyn's older I'll let her watch this particular brand of humor. But there's a problem in America right now, and I happen to be reminded of it every time I watch a show or read a book in which adults are depicted as blathering idiots. We just don't get enough respect.

This might seem a strange way to begin a page of thoughts on helping our children develop a healthy fear of God, but it really isn't such a long stretch if you think about it. After all, 1 John 4:20 tells us that if we don't love the brothers and sisters we can see, how can we love a God we have not seen? I believe that "fear"—also translated as reverence or respect—functions on the same principle: if our children don't know how to show reverence to the people they *can* see, how can we expect them to revere

God, whom they have never seen?

First Peter 2:17 underscores this thought. Peter writes: "Show proper respect to everyone: Love the brotherhood of believers, fear God." Isn't the order intriguing? We are first to respect and love the people we can see. I believe this, then, teaches us how to respect and love the God we can't see.

Psychologists and others have long known that the quality of relationship with our Heavenly Father is often influenced by the quality of relationship with our earthly parents—particularly fathers. A man or woman with an absent, distracted earthly father will often view God as distant or uncaring. Another man or woman who grew up with a critical and harsh father may very well view God as judgmental and punitive.

When NASA builds and launches a space shuttle, they build an exact replica which they do not launch, but keep handy, accessible, and visible on the ground. If there is a mechanical or technical problem with the orbiting shuttle, members of the ground crew seek to work out the bugs on the grounded shuttle they can touch and see before they begin barking instructions across the stratosphere to a shuttle far beyond their grasp or sight.

There is something in the way God established the parent/child relationship that enables us to model for our children that kind of relationship with God. Like the grounded space shuttle, our children get to "practice" with us the relationship skills that will enhance or inhibit their communion with their Heavenly Father. This can be disastrous—if we don't rise to the occasion and accept the responsibility with care. But if we do, it is a beautiful system and unparalleled privilege! Imagine! What joy to play a pivotal role in helping to determine the quality of your child's relationship with the eternal God.

Teaching our children to respect us and other authority figures in their lives is the foundation on which they can begin to build a reverence for God. And reverence for God brings wisdom and—as we are about to discover—life and blessing and righteousness and mercy: Gifts, every one, that outweigh vomit-burgers any day.

Bible Study

As you answer the following questions, keep in mind verses you might want to "pray" over your child. When possible, copy the entire verse from your Bible verbatim or alter it slightly so it includes the name of your child.

Note the parallel between the following verse instructing children to respect their parents and a second verse telling believers to respect their God:

Exodus 20:12: What benefit is reaped by those children who honor their parents? _____

How does this compare with the benefit given in Proverbs 10:27?

_____

What is God's will for our children in their relationship with us as parents?

☐ Colossians 3:20 _____

What is God's will for children in their relationship to Him?

☐ Deuteronomy 11:26-28 _____

☐ Ecclesiastes 12:13 _____

_____

☐ Proverbs 3:7 _____

_____

Read Psalm 34:7-11 and answer the following questions:

ॐ What benefits are promised to those who fear the Lord?

_____

_____

ॐ With what statement does this passage end?

_____

ॐ How might you use this statement as the basis of a prayer for your child? _____

_____

ॐ ॐ ॐ

Prayer Journal

As you pray, spend a few moments in praise, confession, petition, and thanksgiving, incorporating the words of the following Scriptures into your prayers. When appropriate, personalize each verse with the pronouns "I" or "me" or with the name of your child.

Regarding praise:

"I will extol the Lord at all times; His praise will always be on my lips. My soul will boast in the Lord; let the afflicted hear and rejoice. Glorify the Lord with me; let us exalt His name together" (Ps. 34:1-3).

Regarding confession:

"I sought the Lord, and He answered me; He delivered me from all my fears. Those who look to Him are radiant; their faces are never covered with shame" (Ps. 34:4-5).

Regarding our requests to God:

Select one of the verses from the Bible study, and use it as a basis for your intercession regarding the development of patience in your child and even in you as a parent. Which verse did you select? _____

How might you pray this verse for your child?

_____
_____
_____

Additional topics you may want to discuss with God:

&. Are you struggling with cultivating respect in your relationship with your child? Ask God for wisdom. Ask Him for a strategy that will help you encourage your child to respect not only you but other authority figures in his or her life.

&. Respect must be earned. Ask God to reveal to you anything in your life or in your interaction with your child that would undermine his or her respect for you.

⮞ Respect goes two ways. Do you treat your son or daughter with respect? Ask God to show you ways you can model respect to your child by showing respect *for* your child.

⮞ Ask the Holy Spirit to cultivate a deep reverence for God within your child.

❦ ❦ ❦

Regarding thanksgiving:

"How great is Your goodness, which You have stored up for those who fear You, which You bestow in the sight of men on those who take refuge in You" (Ps. 31:19).

❦ ❦ ❦

Space for thoughts, requests, praises, insights, a letter to God, a list of favorite verses on this topic, notes, and/or answers to prayer.

_____
_____
_____
_____
_____
_____
_____
_____
_____
_____
_____
_____
_____
_____
_____
_____
_____
_____
_____
_____
_____

❦ ❦ ❦

Characteristics God Wants to Develop in Your Child

DAY ❧19❧ Joy

"You are to rejoice before the Lord your God in everything you put your hand to" (Deut. 12:18).

What was it about the movie *Hook* that so captivated all of us a few years back? Robin Williams, certainly. And pirates—pirates always help. And of course Tinkerbell because, let's face it, Flying Pixie Dust is a pretty interesting idea. It could be really useful too if someone other than Steven Spielburg created some.

But that warm feeling the movie left us with . . . where did that come from?

Oh, I know. The plot. That really great storyline in which a man rediscovers . . . what was it he rediscovered? Oh, yes.

Joy.

Peter Pan rediscovered joy, and audiences across the nation cheered and cried. He found his lost "happy thoughts" and, for the first time in a long time, knew what it was to fly again. He learned how to laugh and to love again and, in the process, he reclaimed his wife and children.

But it didn't happen overnight, did it? He had to work hard to relearn the art of joy.

Perhaps, when we are children, joy comes to us as a gift. But as we grow into the weight of adult problems and responsibilities, maintaining our joy—or regaining it if we have lost it—demands a conscious effort.

I think joy is not as much a "feeling" as it is a skill. After all, the world certainly presents us with enough muck to bog down almost any emotion based on something as fleeting as a feeling. No, joy is a choice. It's something we learn to do. And once we master the art of joy, it gives wings to everything else in our lives.

Joy also brings us health. No, really! There is something about laughter that releases life-giving hormones into the body. It also releases stress, which can inhibit the immune system.

I don't know about you, but when it comes to *my* child, I don't want something as important as joy to be left to chance. Childhood should be a time of joy—and a time of learning the *skill* of joy so that as an adult, faced with grown-up sized problems and responsibilities, joy remains a much-exercised option.

❦   ❦   ❦

Bible Study

As you answer the following questions, keep in mind verses you might want to "pray" over your child. When possible, copy the entire verse from your Bible verbatim or alter it slightly so it includes the name of your child.

As believers, we have much to be joyful about. What are some of the blessings God has given us for which we are to be joyful?

☐ Psalm 13:5 _____

☐ Psalm 33:21 _____

☐ Jeremiah 15:16 _____

☐ Luke 10:20 _____

☐ John 15:10-11 _____

Is joy an "option" or a commandment? Summarize the following verses:

☐ Psalm 100:1-2 _____

☐ 1 Thessalonians 5:16 _____
☐ Philippians 4:4 _____

Are we only to be joyful in the good times? What do the following verses teach us about choosing joy during tough times?

☐ James 1:2 _____

☐ Luke 6:22-23 _____

☐ 1 Peter 4:13 _____

❦ ❦ ❦

Prayer Journal

As you pray, spend a few moments in praise, confession, petition, and thanksgiving, incorporating the words of the following Scriptures into your prayers. When appropriate, personalize each verse with the pronouns "I" or "me" or with the name of your child.

Regarding praise:

"I will be glad and rejoice in You; I will sing praise to Your name, O Most High" (Ps. 9:2).

❦ ❦ ❦

Regarding confession:

"Therefore, there is now no condemnation for those who are in Christ Jesus" (Rom. 8:1).

❦ ❦ ❦

Regarding our requests to God:

"May the God of hope fill you with all joy and peace as you trust in Him, so that you may overflow with hope by the power of the Holy Spirit" (Rom. 15:13).

How might you pray this verse for your child?

_____

_____

Additional topics you may want to discuss with God:

  ❧ Ask God to make your home a joyful place. Richard Bax-

204

ter wrote: "Keep company with the more cheerful sort of the godly; there is no mirth like the mirth of believers." God *wants* us to have joy—there is nothing godly in dour faces.

&. Ask God to plant joy in the heart of your child. Robert Louis Stevenson observed that "to miss the joy is to miss all."

❦ ❦ ❦

Regarding thanksgiving:

"The Lord is my strength and my shield; my heart trusts in Him, and I am helped. My heart leaps for joy and I will give thanks to Him in song" (Ps. 28:7).

❦ ❦ ❦

Space for thoughts, requests, praises, insights, a letter to God, a list of favorite verses on this topic, notes, and/or answers to prayer.

❦ ❦ ❦

Characteristics God Wants to Develop in Your Child

Steeped in God's Word

"You are in error because you do not know the Scriptures or the power of God" (Matt. 22:29).

During our first year of marriage Larry and I lived in Anderson, Indiana while Larry completed his doctorate. The year brimmed with new experiences for me: marriage, moving away from friends and family in sunny Southern California, and finally—and this was a biggie—living in the country.

Maybe "country" isn't the right word, since we were living in a house in the middle of a housing subdivision filled with other families. But it sure seemed countrified to me! We lived, after all, six miles from town. We passed farms—actual *farms*—on our way into town where Larry taught classes at Anderson College and I worked at a bank. And on the evenings when Larry drove to Ball State University to take his doctoral studies, he left our subdivision, turned onto a tree-lined country road, and didn't pass anything but cornfields for twenty miles until he got to Muncie.

We even had a volunteer fire department.

This might not seem unusual to you, but to a gal born and raised in Southern California, this was revolutionary. After all, I had grown up in a "city" that consumes virtually half its state. Rural had not been in my vocabulary.

On the nights Larry drove to Muncie for classes, I was nervous. Alone, in an unfamiliar house in a strange city and state—and out in the boondocks, no less—I began to let my fears get the best of me. Our little subdivision was so isolated—an island of civilization in a sea of cornfields—wouldn't it make a great target for rapists and robbers?

One evening just after Larry drove away, the doorbell rang. Terrified, I grabbed a butcher knife from the kitchen. Heart racing, I held the knife poised behind my back and cracked open the front door. Ready to defend myself, I peered onto the porch. There, clad in green, stood my nemesis: a cookie-toting girl scout.

This embarrassing incident, however, did little to shake me to my senses. As the nights progressed, I was still afraid.

One evening I became obsessed by the thought that someone would break in and (try not to judge me too harshly here—I was young) put me in the oven. I even opened the oven door and peered in to see if I would fit.

Larry bought me a can of mace—but I was afraid it would just get used on me.

One night a storm blew in. Buffeted on all sides by a howling wind, the little house whistled and rattled and creaked. I began to panic. What was that noise? Was it the wind—or something more sinister? If someone were drawing a glass cutter across a back bedroom window, would I recognize the sound? Or would I assume it was a wind-driven branch scratching at the glass?

I did the only thing an intelligent, fast-thinking, rational young woman could do: I got my butcher knife, backed myself into a corner, and stood frozen with fear for forty-five minutes until I heard my husband's car in the garage.

That did it! Fear was ruining my life. Knives and mace might protect me from a flesh-and-blood intruder, but they were useless when it came to defending myself from my own fear. It was time to get tough and play rough. It was time to break out the heavy artillery.

The next night, Larry reluctantly readied himself for class. "Are you sure you'll be OK?" He asked a dozen times.

"I'm ready this time," I assured as I waved him out the door. "I've got my secret weapon in place."

"Yeah, but last night—"

"Forget last night. I'm in control. I'm ready for the enemy."

Larry probably went to his car wondering how, in a small town in which I barely knew a soul, I'd managed to hook up with a black-market bazooka dealer.

In the kitchen, I began to clear the dinner dishes. Sliding them into the soapy water, I glanced up at the window over the sink. There, framed by the twilight, was an index card taped to the glass. I took a moment to read the words I had copied that afternoon: "For God did not give us a spirit of timidity, but a spirit of power, of love and of self-discipline" (2 Tim. 1:7).

Later, pulling warm laundry from the dryer, I paused to read a card taped to the wall above the appliances: "Let the beloved of the Lord rest secure in Him, for He shields him all day long, and the one the Lord loves rests between His shoulders" (Deut. 33:12).

And still later, as I went to the stereo to insert my favorite cassette, I read: "The Lord is faithful, and will strengthen and protect you from the evil one" (2 Thes. 3:3).

When Larry pulled into the driveway that night around 11, I greeted him at the door with a smile instead of a knife.

The intruder had been conquered: Not by mace, not by cutlery, but by the power of the Word of God. When we begin to catch on to the power inherent in Scripture, our lives will never be the same. If we dare to instill this insight into our children, their lives will be forever changed as well!

🐚 🐚 🐚

Bible Study

As you answer the following questions, keep in mind verses you might want to "pray" over your child. When possible, copy the entire verse from your Bible verbatim or alter it slightly so it includes the name of your child.

According to 2 Timothy 3:16, what is the origin of Scipture? _

_____

What are the situations identified in this verse in which God wants us to be guided by Scripture?

_____

According to 2 Timothy 3:17, what is the result when a man, woman, or child applies the Word of God in his or her life?

_____

What other benefits are ours when we immerse ourselves in the Word of God?

☐ Psalm 19:7-8: The Word of the Lord _____ the soul; makes the simple man or woman _____, brings _____ to the heart, and gives us an _____ perspective.

☐ Psalm 40:8: When God's Word is in our hearts, we will _____

☐ Proverbs 30:5: The Word of God is a _____

☐ Luke 11:28: If we hear the Word of God and obey His Word, we will be _____

☐ Romans 10:17: The Word of God produces within us ____ _____

How much should we value the Holy Scriptures?

☐ Psalms 19:10: King David valued the Word of God more than _____

☐ Job 23:12: Job used what words to describe the values he placed on the Word of God? _____

❦　❦　❦

Prayer Journal

As you pray, spend a few moments in praise, confession, petition, and thanksgiving, incorporating the words of the following Scriptures into your prayers. When appropriate, personalize each verse with the pronouns "I" or "me" or with the name of your child.

Regarding praise:

"Praise be to You, O Lord; teach me Your decrees" (Ps. 119:12).

❦　❦　❦

Regarding confession:

"Direct my footsteps according to Your Word; let no sin rule over me" (Ps. 119:133).

❦　❦　❦

Regarding our requests to God:

"How can a young man keep his way pure? By living according to Your Word. I seek You with all my heart; do not let me stray from Your commands. I have hidden Your Word in my heart that I might not sin against You. Praise be to You, O Lord; teach me Your decrees. With my lips I recount all the laws that come from Your mouth. I rejoice in following Your statutes as one rejoices in great riches. I meditate on Your precepts and consider Your ways. I delight in Your decrees; I will not neglect Your Word" (Ps. 119:9-16).

Use this verse as a basis for your intercession regarding your child's attitude about God's Word.

How might you pray this verse for your child?

_____
_____
_____
_____
_____
_____

Additional topics you may want to discuss with God:

🍂 Ask God to develop, within your child, a love for Scripture. If your child doesn't have his or her own Bible, in a user-friendly translation, make this purchase as soon as possible.

🍂 Talk to God about the kind of example you should be for your child. How much time do you spend in the Scriptures? Does your child see how you apply God's Word in your life?

🍂 Ask God to reveal opportunities to apply His Word to real-life problems faced by members of your family. Ask Him to help you remember to look to the Bible for comfort or direction when confronted by a problem in your family or in the life of your child. In response to a problem, select and memorize an appropriate verse.

Regarding thanksgiving:
"Parise our God, all you His servants, you who fear Him, both small and great!" (Rev. 19:5)

❦   ❦   ❦

Space for thoughts, requests, praises, insights, a letter to God, a list of favorite verses on this topic, notes, and/or answers to prayer.

_____

_____

_____

_____

_____

_____

_____

_____

_____

_____

_____

_____

_____

_____

_____

_____

_____

_____

_____

_____

_____

_____

_____

_____

_____

_____

❦   ❦   ❦

Characteristics God Wants to Develop in Your Child

DAY ❧21❧ | ## Committed to Prayer

"One day Jesus was praying in a certain place. When He finished, one of His disciples said to Him, 'Lord, teach us to pray.'"
Luke 11:1

Today we're going to pray that our children would develop hearts bent toward prayer. But before we do, let me congratulate you: You have already increased the likelihood that your child—particularly if he or she is still living at home—will recognize the value of prayer and incorporate it into his or her life.

And you have accomplished this through the power of your example as a parent who prays.

❧ Mark Bellinger knows this is true. You may remember that I mentioned him and his wife Nancy earlier in the book. Mark begins each morning in prayer, kneeling by the living room couch, talking to God about the day's events and about each member of his family.

One morning, however, Mark found it hard to concentrate. It was the Saturday morning following an evening Mark had put his seventeen-year-old son Craig on restriction for breaking curfew. The house was quiet and Mark's prayer time should have gone smoothly. But as he prayed, he couldn't shake the sense that God was sending him a disturbing message. He became convinced that God was asking him to reverse Craig's restriction!

Mark dismissed the feeling and tried to continue with his prayers. Again, he felt the Holy Spirit stirring in his soul. God was saying: "You just finished praying and telling Me you want to walk in My will, but you're not listening to Me!"

Mark remembers, "I argued with God. I reminded Him that I

never go back on my word—especially when it comes to discipline, and my kids know it. I'm not harsh, but I'm fair, and when I make a decision, my kids know there's no arguing or getting around it. But that day, the feeling wouldn't go away. God wanted Craig off restriction."

Mark called Craig into the living room. Perplexed, he shook his head. "Son, this'll be a first," he said slowly. "As I was praying, I felt God telling me to let you off restriction. He told me to tell you that He overruled my decision. He told me that I'm the head of this house, but that He's the head of me."

Craig didn't whoop or yell or cheer. Instead, his eyes welled with tears. "Dad, I knew you wouldn't change your mind so I didn't say anything, but this weekend is the church youth retreat and I really wanted to go. So I stayed up half the night praying that God would speak to you. I knew that if it was His will for me to go to the retreat, He would somehow let you change your mind and let me go."

Praying parents reap children who pray.

ਇ The Loftin family is another example. Twenty years ago, J.P. and Betty Loftin prayed fervently for their thirteen-year-old son Henry who was running with a crowd of boys involved in alcohol and pornography. Every Sunday afternoon for three years, J.P. and Betty gathered with committed friends from church and spent the hour in prayer for Henry.

Henry never knew about his parents' prayers until he was reunited with God. But the hindsight into what his parents had accomplished for him through spiritual warfare left a strong impression. Henry knew he had been the beneficiary of the power of his parents' prayers. Today, he is committed to giving that same gift to his seven-year-old daughter, Tabitha. Each morning he prays Galatians 5:22 as he asks God to harvest the fruit of the Spirit in the life of his little girl.

Will Tabitha come to realize the power of prayer through the example of her parents and grandparents? There is a good chance she will. What a beautiful heritage!

ਇ Finally, do you remember Chris and Debbie and their daughter, Ashley? The prayer reminder cards crafted by Debbie and Ashley generated a greater response than anyone dared hope. Before long, Debbie began receiving requests for more cards. Entire adults' and children's Sunday School classes were distributing the cards and praying against the cancer found in Ashley. Friends began mailing cards to out-of-state friends and family. Still others were taking cards to support groups and Bible studies. Before long, Ashley's cards were on desks, refrigerators, and in Bibles throughout Southern California and even across the state line.

Two years after Debbie had collapsed, weeping, in my living room over the bitter news of Ashley's cancer, the treatments ended. Ashley's final round of chemotherapy was a time for exhausted jubilation and thanksgiving. Eight-year-old Ashley was given a clean bill of health. And to anyone who would listen, Ashley herself was ready with the reason why:

"I got healed of cancer," she said a hundred times if she said it once: "Know how? Chemotherapy, radiation, and *prayer.*"

Ashley knows the power of her parents' prayers—and the prayers of other believers too. And this knowledge has borne much fruit in her life.

"I wouldn't wish this kind of experience on anyone," Debbie says today. "But there's no denying that God used the horrendous experiences of those two years to change our lives. When I hear Ashley pray today, I'm amazed. She's ten now, and her prayers still reflect a depth that makes me want to cry. She's been through a lot, and she knows that prayer is what brought her through the worst of it."

Do you want your child to wield the power of prayer in his or her own life? If so, you're on the right track. Just keep praying.

If you haven't already done so, look for ways to let your child know that you are praying for him or her. Ask your son or daughter for prayer requests that you can bring to God. Write a note—"I'm praying for you today"—and drop it in your son's lunch bag. Follow up your prayers by asking your son or daughter for updates on the problem they asked you to pray about. When God answers, thank Him together.

John Bunyan described prayer as "a shield to the soul, a sacrifice to God, and a scourge to Satan."

William Law put it another way: "He who has learned how to pray has learned the greatest secret of a holy and happy life."

Finally, Louis Evans has observed that "the man who kneels to God can stand up to anything."

You *can* influence your child toward his or her own commitment to prayer — all it takes is your prayers and your example. Yet what an opportunity! On your knees, you have the power to equip your child for life — real life — in the very greatest sense of the word.

❦   ❦   ❦

Bible Study

As you answer the following questions, keep in mind verses you might want to "pray" over your child. When possible, copy the entire verse from your Bible verbatim or alter it slightly so it includes the name of your child.

You have spent the past weeks not only in prayer, but in the Word of God. What promise is yours as you continue to immerse yourself in prayer and in the Word of God?
  ☐ John 15:7-8 _____

How might you pray this verse for your child?
_____
_____
_____

Abraham believed that God would give him a son even when all the evidence in the natural world shouted that Abraham was past the age of having any children at all. He not only believed God's promise that he would one day be a father; he also believed God when God promised he would do great things in the lives of Abraham's offspring.
  ☐ What does Romans 4:20-21 say about Abraham's faith in the promises of God? _____
_____
_____

215

God has already blessed you and me with children. Yet, like Abraham, we are believing that God will do great things in the lives of our children. What do the following verses tell us about God's ability to bring about that which He has promised or planned?
☐ Isaiah 46:11 _____

_____

☐ Hebrews 10:23 _____

_____

When the challenges of parenting in the '90s seem overwhelming, you and I can be encouraged by the fact that, in our own strength, we really *are* insufficient. If this seems an odd truth from which to draw encouragement, think again.
☐ What was Paul's perspective on weakness, as explained in 2 Corinthians 12:9? _____

_____

_____

And when we worry about being less than perfect parents, how can we bridge the gap between who we are and what we desire to be?
☐ Philippians 4:13 _____

_____

_____

Prayer Journal

As you pray, spend a few moments in praise, confession, petition, and thanksgiving, incorporating the words of the following Scriptures into your prayers. When appropriate, personalize each verse with the pronouns "I" or "me" or with the name of your child.

Regarding praise:
"Give thanks to the Lord Almighty, for the Lord is good; His love endures forever" (Jer. 33:11).

Regarding confession:
"The Lord our God is merciful and forgiving" (Dan. 9:9).

❦ ❦ ❦

Regarding our requests to God:
"May the Lord answer you when you are in distress; may the name of the God of Jacob protect you. May He send you help from the sanctuary and grant you support from Zion. May He remember all your sacrifices and accept your burnt offerings. May He give you the desire of your heart and make all your plans succeed" (Ps. 20:1-4).

How might you pray this verse for your child? _____

_____

_____

_____

❦ ❦ ❦

Regarding thanksgiving:
"Now to Him who is able to do immeasurably more than all we ask or imagine, according to His power that is at work within us, to Him be glory in the church and in Christ Jesus throughout all generations, forever and ever! Amen" (Eph. 3:20-21).

❦ ❦ ❦

Space for thoughts, requests, praises, insights, a letter to God, a list of favorite verses on this topic, notes, and/or answers to prayer.

_____

_____

_____

_____

_____

_____

_____

_____

❦ ❦ ❦

More Prayers for Children

The Bible verses examined in the previous pages are powerful. They are made even more powerful by the fact that you have just spent three weeks knitting them, by your prayers, into the very fabric of your life and the lives of your children.

But don't stop now!

Your adventures as a parent warrior are just beginning! I encourage you to continue honing and wielding the great spiritual weaponry available to you in the form of prayer and Scripture:

❧ Submit daily your own heart and soul to the purifying scrutiny of the Holy Spirit, even as you submit your children to His care and guidance.

❧ Search the Bible for verses and passages that verbalize your heartfelt desires for your children. If you don't already have one, purchase a topical Bible and use it to quickly locate verses that pertain to struggles and issues relevent to you and to your family.

❧ Personalize these passages and verses in your prayers. Use first-person pronouns when applying the verse to your own life; insert the name of your son or daughter when "praying" the verse for them.

In the following pages, I've compiled a list of scriptural prayers for children. Some of them were offered by parents for their biological children; others were penned by the Apostle Paul as he prayed for his "spiritual children"—the men and women he helped birth into the kingdom of God. Still others were written by Peter and the unknown author of Hebrews.

Use these verses. Personalize them. Pray them over your children. Use whatever blank spaces and pages are available to jot down other verses you discover on your own—verses that speak to you about you or your child and have found their way into your prayer life.

Biblical Accounts of Parents' Prayers for Their Children
In each of the following passages, parents make requests to God for their children. Although these stories don't detail actual prayers that today's

218

parents might adopt for their own children, I believe they still offer much in the way of instruction and encouragement:

Genesis 17:18 — Abraham prays that Ishmael might be blessed.

Job 1:5 — Job regularly prayed for each of his ten children.

Matthew 15:22-28 — Canaanite woman seeks prayer for demon-possessed daughter; her request is granted because of her faith.

Matthew 17:14-18 — Man seeks healing for his son.

The following passages describe David's prayers for his son, Solomon, and are well-suited for adoption into your prayers for your children:

1 Chronicles 22:11-12 — David prays for Solomon's leadership skills.

1 Chronicles 28:9 — David prays again for Solomon

1 Chronicles 29:19 — David prays for Solomon on the day before his coronation.

Prayers for Spiritual Children

As you continue in your role as Parent Warrior, consider spending a day or more on each of the following passages. Each passage has much to offer as you incorporate it into your prayers for your children:

Romans 15:13

2 Corinthians 13:7, 11, 14

Ephesians 1:15-19

Ephesians 3:14-19

Philippians 1:3-5; 9-10

Philippians 2:15

Colossians 1:3

Colossians 1:9

Colossians 2:1-2

Colossians 4:2

1 Thessalonians 3:12-13

1 Thessalonians 5:23

2 Thessalonians 1:11

2 Thessalonians 2:16-17

2 Thessalonians 3:5, 16

2 Timothy 1:3

2 Timothy 2:1

2 Timothy 2:7

Philemon 4, 6

Hebrews 13:20-21

1 Peter 5:10

Thanksgiving Log

(These pages may be reproduced for your personal use)

Request:
Answer(s) (including dates):

_____

_____

_____

_____

Request:
Answer(s) (including dates):

_____

_____

_____

_____

Request:
Answer(s) (including dates):

_____

_____

_____

_____

Request:
Answer(s) (including dates):

_____

_____

_____

_____

Request:
Answer(s) (including dates):

_____

_____

_____

_____

Request:
Answer(s) (including dates):

_____

_____

_____

_____

Request:
Answer(s) (including dates):

_____

_____

_____

_____

Request:
Answer(s) (including dates):

_____

_____

_____

_____

Request:
Answer(s) (including dates):

_____

_____

_____

_____

Request:
Answer(s) (including dates):

_____

_____

_____

_____

Request:
Answer(s) (including dates):

_____

_____

_____

_____

Request:
Answer(s) (including dates):

_____

_____

_____

_____

Request:
Answer(s) (including dates):

_____

_____

_____

_____

Request:
Answer(s) (including dates):

_____

_____

_____

_____

Request:
Answer(s) (including dates):

_____

_____

_____

_____

Request:
Answer(s) (including dates):

_____

_____

_____

_____

Karen Scalf Linamen is a freelance writer and popular speaker for women's groups. A former editor with Focus on the Family, she has written or cowritten seven books and several hundred articles. She loves hearing from readers. To reach her, write:

Karen Linamen
P.O. Box 2673
Duncanville, TX 75138

E-mail: klinamen@flash.net